Adventures in Parenthood

By Denise Van Outen and available from Headline:
Bumpalicious: How to Relax and Enjoy Your Pregnancy

DENISE VAN OUTEN

with Sam Mann

Adventures in Parenthood

headline

All photographs from the personal collection of Denise Van Outen, except page 92, courtesy of Claire Dundas.

The right of Denise Van Outen to be identified as the Author of the Work has been asserted by her in accordance with the Copyright, Designs and Patents Act 1988.

First published in 2012

by HEADLINE PUBLISHING GROUP

1

Cataloguing in Publication Data is available from the British Library

978 0 7553 6202 8

Typeset in Sabon and Formata by Perfect Bound Limited, London

Printed and bound in Great Britain by Clays Ltd, St Ives plc

Headline's policy is to use papers that are natural, renewable and recyclable products and made from wood grown in sustainable forests. The logging and manufacturing processes are expected to conform to the environmental regulations of the country of origin.

HEADLINE PUBLISHING GROUP
An Hachette UK Company
338 Euston Road
London NW1 3BH

www.headline.co.uk
www.hachette.co.uk

Contents

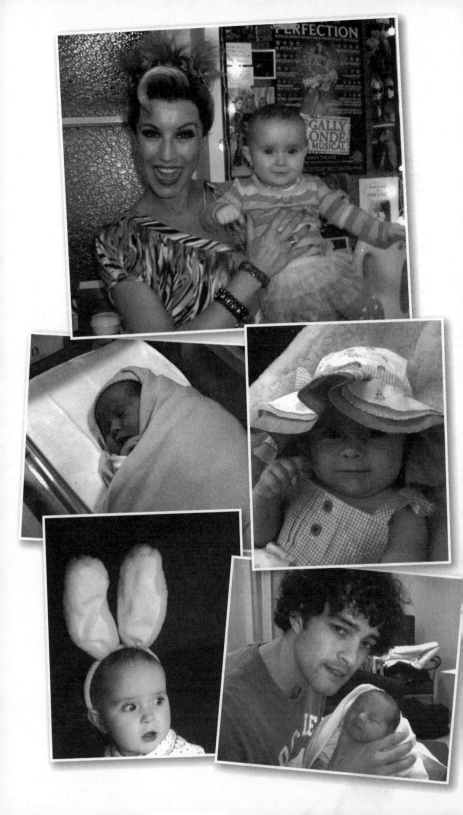

Foreword

No amount of reading magazines and baby books came close to preparing me for the first few weeks of motherhood, and if I'm honest, even now – two years on – I still get plenty of curve balls and surprises thrown my way. Becoming a mum has made me appreciate the support and love of my friends and family more than ever.

As a first-time mum wrapped up in my baby bubble, it was easy to forget there are millions of parents out there who have been through it all and are willing to share their invaluable experience. It wasn't until I posted a dilemma on Twitter and received an overwhelming response, that I realised just how supportive other mums (and dads) can be. Since then I have turned to tweeting about mummy matters on many occasions and found my followers to be a huge source of advice and encouragement.

I hope by reading about my two emotional, fun-filled years as a mum, along with some of the personal experiences of my fabulous Twitter followers, you will feel the same sense of camaraderie, not to mention benefit from some of our hard-won knowledge. Above all, I hope this book will help you enjoy your own magical adventures in parenthood.

Love, Denise x

Chapter 1

Hello Baby

For as long as I can remember I've dreamt about meeting an amazing man, marrying him and having two children. It was as if I always knew it would happen one day and, even as a young girl, I'd fantasise about carrying out the duties that come with being a mum – changing nappies, cooking, playing in the park and giving plenty of cuddles. Even through my heady teens and twenties when the only thing I was capable of nursing was a permanent hangover, I just assumed my life would take a certain path: I would have my fun, meet the man of my dreams, settle down, have kids and live happily ever after. I had a couple of false starts on the man front before I met Lee in 2007, but as soon as we got together I knew I'd finally found 'the one'. So, at the age of thirty-four I was on course. That was, until I had a health MOT in 2008...

I'd never considered for a second that I might not be able to have kids of my own. But when, as a routine procedure, the doctor tested my ovarian reserve and told me it was considerably low for someone my age, it knocked me for six. He explained that it didn't mean I couldn't have children but it could take some time to conceive. I would also need to consider that my fertility would continue to decrease as time went on. He recommended that if I was in a stable relationship and we were certain we wanted children, we should start trying to conceive straight away.

Wow! For the very first time I was forced to face the fact that despite all my dreaming it may not be possible for me to have children. For a couple of days I moped around the flat feeling sorry for myself and a bit stupid for just assuming that one day I would become a mum. Lee was fantastic and reassured me that we would do everything we could to become parents and that meant cracking on with it as soon as we were married. We decided to tie the knot sooner rather than later and on 25 April 2009, after a manic few months of preparation, we became husband and wife in an emotional ceremony on a stunning island in the Seychelles.

After the wedding I did everything I could to increase my chances of falling pregnant. I left my job at Capital Radio, which cut my workload considerably, and kick-started a health and fitness regime. I am terrible when it comes to motivating myself to exercise and I have a little voice in my head that tells me just one cupcake won't harm, so I knew I'd need help. I called on the expert advice of my good friend and personal trainer Nicki Waterman and top dietician Amanda Ursell. If you have read my pregnancy book *Bumpalicious* then you will have heard all about my efforts to knock myself into shape.

As well as pounding the streets with Nicki I also embarked on another, more dramatic way to get fit: I joined a group of celebrities climbing Mount Kilimanjaro, the highest mountain in Africa, to raise money for Comic Relief. I'd been personally asked by Gary Barlow to take part so I would have been mad to turn him down, plus my good friend Fearne Cotton was taking part – along with Cheryl Cole, Kimberley Walsh and Ronan Keating – so there was no doubt it was going to be a lot of fun. Having a goal to focus on kept me motivated to keep up my training when I'd rather have been curled up on the sofa eating chocolate biscuits and feeling sorry for myself.

A couple of weeks before the climb I was faced with loads of interviews and as per usual the press weren't interested in asking me about what I was promoting – the climb and Comic Relief – but instead just focused on my personal life. It felt like every journalist ended with the killer question: 'When are you and Lee planning to start a family?' I gave the same answer to each of them: 'When the time is right – you'll have to wait and see,' with a smile on my face, of course. This despite the fact that the honest answer would have been: 'Your guess is as good as mine. I may not even be able to have children and the thought of that is making me feel awful, so let's move on!'

I survived the press interviews and went on to make it to the top of Mount Kili, which was amazing. The training and healthy diet paid off and I felt in the best shape I'd ever been. Then suddenly everything changed: I was exhausted and felt sick for a couple of weeks. It all culminated in me feeling terrible while at a friend's BBQ one Sunday afternoon shortly after I got back. I had eaten a burger and had drunk a couple of glasses of rosé, so I put it down to the fact my body wasn't used to the greasy food and alcohol any more after my recent health kick. That said, I had been tucking into cheese like it was going out of fashion – morning, noon and night, I couldn't help but pop to the fridge and grab a slice.

That evening I was having trouble sleeping and at 4 am I sat bolt upright – and suddenly I just knew. I was pregnant! I woke Lee up and while he was gradually coming round I found the pregnancy test I had stashed in my drawer. Now please let me stress that I normally pee in private but this was a special occasion and I don't think wild horses would have kept Lee from being part of the moment. We held hands so tightly as we watched two pink lines appear on the white stick before bouncing around the bedroom with delight. After five months of trying and worrying we were pregnant!

Nine Months and Counting

I can't say being pregnant was quite as I had imagined. The early months weren't too bad as it was still a novelty – I enjoyed receiving lots of attention, having my bags carried and being offered a seat wherever I went – but towards the end it seemed like I had been pregnant for years and I couldn't wait to feel lighter on my feet and meet our little girl. It was a bit like watching a film when you've already read the book – you know the plot so you want to skip to the ending – only my fast-forward button didn't work!

Antenatal classes run by the NCT (National Childbirth Trust) came highly recommended by many of my mates as they felt it prepared them much more than just reading pregnancy books. They also made lots of friends at the classes who they met up with on a weekly basis once their babies were born, usually in Starbucks or Costa where they'd take over the place with pushchairs and screaming newborns. I really liked the idea of meeting other women whose babies were due around the same time as ours, but unfortunately Lee was touring around the UK in an Oscar Wilde play for the majority of my pregnancy and the last thing I wanted was to be the one person on her own at the NCT class, surrounded by happy couples sat entwined on birthing balls. So I decided to make alternative arrangements.

Thankfully I managed to find a great lady, Becky, who came to the flat to give us classes that fitted round our schedules, on Lee's days off. Funnily enough, she started running the classes after experiencing the same problem when she was pregnant, as she too is married to an actor. The sessions were great and we covered so much – including how to identify when you are in labour (which may sound bizarre but my mate spent two days waiting for the terrible diarrhoea she was certain would follow the painful stomach cramps she'd been having!), breathing techniques and pain-relief options. We spent lots of time practising changing nappies and the best way to hold a baby by using a plastic doll, which to be honest felt very weird at times. Once we'd completed the course I felt ready for anything. Well, almost...

Six days before my due date I felt a dull ache close to my pubic bone. As the pain got worse throughout the day I decided to call my obstetrician, and after describing what I was feeling he asked me to go in and see him straight away. He checked me over then told me he wasn't happy with the way Betsy was sitting. It seemed I would need to have a Caesarean. At first I thought, 'Great, I've spent the last nine months preparing to push Betsy out and mastering the art of controlled breathing and now I don't need any of it!' But when I'd had more time to put it into perspective I realised the important thing was that now I could be sure Betsy would arrive safe and sound. And with an added bonus ... pain-free!

Here at Last

On 1 May 2010 Betsy was born at the Portland Hospital in central London. It wasn't all plain sailing, thanks to a last-minute panic attack on my part. I'd read hundreds of magazines and books over the previous nine months and could hold court on anything to do with pregnancy and giving birth. But when push came to shove (excuse the pun), all I could think about was what I had seen on a TV series called *One Born Every Minute*, which follows the stories of women in labour. If you've seen it I'm sure you'll agree that some of the episodes are probably not the best point of reference if you're just about to have a baby yourself. But as much as I tried to steer clear of it, I couldn't help myself, and the images were now coming back to haunt me in droves.

Thankfully, despite my last-minute panic, the whole procedure went well and there was no drama like I'd witnessed on the TV show. Like most women having planned Caesareans I had an epidural, which meant I remained totally aware of everything that was happening but didn't feel any pain, so I managed to keep smiling throughout. Lee was a massive tower of strength and took it all in his stride while looking dashingly handsome in his surgical scrubs as if he'd just walked off the set of a hospital drama. He was making the most of his supporting role, snapping away with his camera and playing DJ with the playlist we'd spent hours compiling especially for the occasion.

I couldn't quite believe it when I heard Betsy cry for the first time after the doctor lifted her out of me. Before then, hearing a baby cry would wind me up but Betsy's cry was genuinely lovely to hear. I couldn't wait to hold her. The midwife passed her to me wrapped in a blanket, and as I looked into her beautiful grey eyes for the very first time, I was totally smitten. She had a mop of dark curly hair and even though it's often impossible to tell one newborn from another, there was no denying that Lee was her dad. Her lips were full and kissable, so much so that Lee and I nicknamed them the Portland Pout – I couldn't help but feel a teeny bit jealous.

I must admit I was grateful that she had been cleaned up by the midwife so I could see her features properly. I'd seen pictures of babies covered in a greasy white coating immediately after they've been born (the white vernix) and they look like they're not ready to face the outside world yet! Betsy looked beautiful and so tiny, but with her face all crumpled I couldn't help but notice a slight resemblance to a Shar Pei dog. It didn't worry me though – I knew she would iron out, so to speak. At the twenty-eight-week mark in my pregnancy I'd had one of those 3D scans, which are pretty amazing: you get to see your baby's face while they're still in the womb. I'd kept the picture by my bedside so we could have little face-to-face conversations (all one-way of course) on the lead-up to her arrival, so I actually recognised Betsy from the photo and felt like we knew each other already. I kissed her on the head and whispered, 'Hello, my darling.' Nothing will ever beat that moment of holding Betsy for the first time, with Lee wrapping his arms around both of us. At last I had my own little family.

It was a relief to feel such an instant attachment to Betsy because I had read that some new mums find it hard to bond with their babies at first. A couple of days after Betsy arrived one of the nurses told me there was a mum on another ward who was finding it hard to connect with her newborn and had spent the last few days in floods of tears. I really felt for her – it must be absolutely heartbreaking.

As for me, in those first few moments immediately after the birth I felt something close to euphoria. I didn't want to let Betsy go; she fitted in my arms perfectly. But I could see Lee out of the corner of my eye itching to hold her so I carefully passed her over for her first daddy cuddle. He seemed so natural with her and as his eyes welled up, I could tell he was in love. It felt so right for both of us. When I'd held my niece and nephews as newborn babies I had worried whether I was holding them correctly and I had felt a bit clumsy. With Betsy it seemed like the most natural thing on earth.

I spent five nights in hospital in total as I wanted to rest after my Caesarean and have a few more days secure in the knowledge there were plenty of professionals around to help me. My time at the Portland allowed me to clear up all the worries and questions I had, although the poor nurses must have felt like screaming as I asked them for the hundredth time whether I had enough blankets over Betsy or whether I'd wrapped her up too snugly. Getting Betsy's temperature right was one thing I was really worried about in the early days – I'd read so many books warning new mums of the danger of overheating their babies and the links to cot death. I'm sure when Betsy is talking properly she'll have a whole list of things she's itching to get off her chest and the fact I made her shiver or sweat buckets as a baby is bound to be on it.

I was very grateful to have the extra days in hospital but I know every mum is different. One friend gave birth a week early on the morning of her sister's wedding and, not wanting to miss the big day, she and the baby headed straight to the ceremony to surprise everyone. You have to admire her get up and go! A lot depends on your personal disposition: I was feeling nervous about stepping back into the big wide world as a mum, but I have plenty of friends who couldn't wait to get home once their baby was born. And of course not all hospitals are as comfortable as the Portland. A couple of my friends couldn't wait to discharge themselves from hospital the day after giving birth as they couldn't stand being cooped up behind a drab curtain and having to struggle with their baby alone during the night after their partners were sent home. I certainly don't know how I would have coped for the first few nights without Lee there to help out – I realise I was extremely fortunate to be in a place where partners are allowed to stay in the room. Lee was with us every night with the exception of one – when he was ordered by the production department at the theatre he was working in to get a proper night's sleep. He had been in final rehearsals for his new role in the West End musical *Wicked* and had forgotten some of his lines. Poor thing, he was thoroughly exhausted.

In fact I don't know what I would have done at all without Lee those first few days. He was my knight in shining armour, looking after his two girls and taking on the role of chief nappy changer. I watched him each time he changed Betsy: he was so gentle and looked like he had been doing it for ages. However, there was a little hiccup on day two when he opened Betsy's nappy to find some meconium, the sticky greeny-black tar-like substance that comes from the intestinal tract of newborns. Despite Becky warning us about its appearance during our antenatal classes Lee had completely forgotten all about it. I almost popped a couple of stitches as Lee reeled backwards, gasping: 'No way! What the hell is that? Is she all right? It's like something out of an alien movie!' The nurses were laughing along with me too. When I reminded him it was perfectly healthy he calmed down and the colour soon came back to his cheeks.

Budding Fashionista

I think all first-time mums love the idea of dressing their newborn baby, especially if they have girls, and it's a natural progression from playing with dolls as a child – you could say it's what we were training for. I love my fashion and had been thinking about all the lovely things I would put Betsy in when she got bigger, from fairy wings to princess tutus. The very first outfit she wore was a tiny babygrow with ducks all over it that Fearne Cotton had bought us. It was super-cute and in fact the only outfit out of the huge selection I'd packed for the hospital that fitted her. Despite Betsy weighing in at a healthy 7 lb 10 oz all the newborn outfits were massive on her – how big do they expect newborns to be nowadays? Another job for super daddy: Lee dashed to Mothercare to buy some early baby clothes so we had something to dress her in until she beefed up a little.

The first few days were crazy as visitors came and went, all desperate for a Betsy cuddle. All of our immediate families came, including grandparents and siblings, and Betsy was passed around as though she were a parcel at a kid's birthday party. It was so moving to see everyone cooing over her. My wonderful eighteen-year-old goddaughter Elicia popped in too. She's my best friend's daughter and we have a great relationship. I've been there every step of the way since she was born – babysitting her, celebrating her birthdays, watching her perform in her first theatre production at school and having fun together on countless holidays. My dream is that one day Betsy and Elicia will have the same closeness that we share and I hoped that by asking Elicia to be Betsy's godmother it would strengthen their bond. Elicia was over the moon and it was a good few minutes before the tears stopped flowing. We also asked Lee's best friend Ross, who was best man at our wedding, to be Betsy's godfather.

On the night that Lee had to stay away, my mum kept me company and we had a girly evening together, ordering in pizza and cooing over Betsy. She is definitely one loved little girl and I feel incredibly lucky to have such strong support around me – it made those first few days such a special time.

Smile for the Camera

As our time at the Portland came to an end, Lee and I had to make a decision about how we would deal with the press and the photographers who had been camping outside the hospital for days. Of course this isn't something most parents have to worry about but Lee and I are used to being followed by paparazzi and with Betsy now in the equation we needed to make sure we handled the situation well. Our natural feeling was to protect Betsy by concocting a plan to slip out the back door, as the last thing I wanted was to have a load of cameras shoved in Betsy's or my face. The Portland are used to celebrities slipping in and out and have an underground drop-off and pick-up point so even the most high-profile celebrity can come and go unnoticed. But we knew that sneaking out would only be a short-term solution and wouldn't stop photographers waiting outside our flat. Of course we were aware that people would be interested in seeing Betsy and I do believe that if you live your life in the public eye you can't expect to just switch the attention off when it suits. There would also no doubt be times in the future when I would like to take Betsy to an event or concert, especially when Lee is performing, and I didn't want to have to worry about who would be looking.

We finally decided, therefore, to have a picture taken of the three of us together in a more controlled environment than on a doorstep and so we invited a photographer into our room at the hospital to take the first official photo. We arranged it so that if magazines wanted to use it they had to pay in the form of a donation to Great Ormond Street Children's Hospital in London. It's such a wonderful place and the work they do there is outstanding. I have visited quite a few times over the years since being in the public eye to spend some time with the children, especially over Christmas, and I find the staff, kids and their families a huge inspiration. I was also aware that my obstetrician Pat O'Brien, who delivered Betsy, does amazing work at

GOSH. He was part of a team of surgeons who successfully separated conjoined twins and while I was pregnant he would fill me in on their progress. Later I watched the documentary that followed the whole story. I was in awe of Pat, his fellow surgeons and the amazing work they do, the strength of the twins and their family, and I felt overwhelmed with gratitude for the safe arrival of our own healthy baby daughter.

With the photo situation dealt with, it was time to leave the hospital and say goodbye to the fantastic nurses. I'd grown quite attached to my little room, not to mention very used to the luxury of being cooked for every day! As everyone turned out en masse to say goodbye and wish us luck for the future I felt a mixture of sadness and excitement. Our next adventure was about to begin!

A word from my Twitter followers

Alex, mum to a five-month-old daughter

I decided in my fat, uncomfortable, emotional state of mind that watching a birthing programme would prepare me for my upcoming event. Until then the only thought about giving birth I had had was that if my mum could do it, so could I. Big mistake! I phoned my mum at work screaming hysterically, 'Do you know where babies come out?' Obviously I knew this but it hadn't really sunk in that I would have to actually do it myself. I had started to hope the stories of storks and cabbage patches were true!

Lynne, mum to a twenty-six-year-old son

Giving birth was the most rewarding experience I have ever been through. I was in labour for sixteen and a half hours and I remember every minute of it! It was a Saturday morning and my midwife and I were playing along to a quiz on Radio One. I got forty-six points! When my son Giuseppe was born I had this overwhelming love for this little baby and I love him more every day if that's possible.

Kate, mum to a five-year-old daughter

I was twenty-nine weeks when I noticed a damp patch in my bed. I put it down to the baby pressing on my bladder and went to work as usual. Throughout the morning I kept noticing damp patches so I went to the labour ward for a check-up. They kept me in overnight and the next morning the midwife took one look at me and called the doctor. An examination revealed that I was five centimetres dilated so I was rushed to the delivery suite. Forty-five minutes later my daughter Louisa was born weighing 3 lb 1 oz. She was perfect but tiny so she was kept in for five weeks. I was diagnosed with an incompetent cervix, which meant it couldn't hold the weight of the baby, so I was given a simple stitch to prevent the same thing happening again. I've since had my son Joe, who arrived at forty-two weeks and weighed a healthy 9 lb 11oz – so I've experienced both ends of the scale.

Loren, mum to a five-month-old daughter

I absolutely hated pregnancy, but loved labour! It was the most awful pain, but beautiful at the same time. I'm usually a drama queen so I shocked my boyfriend, mum and nana, who were all there, by not screaming or swearing once.

Belinda, mum to a two-month-old son

I had my little boy at a birth clinic and it was the quickest labour ever. I arrived at 11 am and gave birth thirty-six minutes later. The midwives were rather shocked at how fast it was but it was great to only be in pain for half an hour!

Debbie, mum to a sixteen-year-old son

I was given a pessary to get things going but the midwife told me it was unlikely to work the first time. After ten minutes I was in a lot of pain but the midwife said I was experiencing Braxton Hicks contractions. After another five minutes of excruciating pain she examined me and found that I was ten centimetres dilated. I was put in a wheelchair and wheeled to a lift to take me down to the delivery suite. My son couldn't wait though and as the doors opened I felt him coming. So I put my leg over the side of the wheelchair and out he came!

Hayley, mum to a fourteen-month-old son

I was rushed into hospital at twenty-six weeks when my waters started to come away. It was my first baby so I was petrified! The hospital wasn't equipped for such an early arrival so we were taken to another one where I was monitored for five days until I had nothing left to keep the baby in. I gave birth to my son Rocco via a C-section and after spending thirteen weeks in three different hospitals I was sent home with my gorgeous little boy.

Charlotte, mum to a four-year-old son

My favourite photo is of me holding my son for the first time. I look a state – my hair is puffed up, I'm wearing the hospital maternity smock and I've got a catheter in – but I have the biggest, widest grin on my face. I can't express how much I love that photo and I well up every time I look at it. I fed him shortly after the photo was taken – the feelings running through my veins were unbelievable and my hair was standing on end.

Hannah, mum of three

I already had two boys aged seven and nine when I found out I was pregnant for the third time. I received excellent care and gave birth to my daughter at home while my mum and my boys were in the next room. My best friend acted as midwife.

Claire, mum to a two-month-old daughter

My wonderful midwife handed our daughter to my boyfriend once she'd cleaned her up and he announced we had a little girl. I couldn't believe it as I was convinced we were having a boy! He then held her by my face so that I could see her and

I couldn't believe how familiar she looked. It felt like I'd known her my whole life. Strangely, although I'd been convinced I was having a boy all through my pregnancy, I had a dream a few days before she was born that I had a little girl with lots of dark hair and that's exactly what she looked like.

Chapter 2

There's No Place Like Home

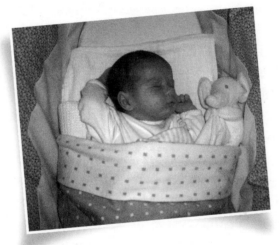

M y emotions on leaving the hospital were the strangest I have ever experienced. I went from being in the very capable hands of the amazing nurses at the Portland Hospital – who were on hand 24/7 to answer any problems or questions I had – to suddenly being out in the big, bad world on my own (or at least that's what it felt like). I was scared rigid. The only thing I can equate it to is the opening night at the theatre, when I'm always a bag of nerves and just kind of switch on to autopilot. But this was times a million!

I'd been told there were loads of paparazzi waiting outside the front of the hospital so I left through the back door. Betsy was in a cute little outfit and I'd brushed my hair and put some makeup on because I wanted to make an effort for the occasion. It was such a glorious day, the sun was shining and there wasn't a cloud in the sky, which I took as a sign of good things to come. Lee was at a dress rehearsal for his musical *Wicked* so he couldn't be there to take us home. Bless him, he was really upset as he wanted so much to be with us, but there was no way he could miss the rehearsal as the show opened in two days. I would have loved him to have been there too but completely understood, and because we had discussed it well in advance I had time to get my head around stepping out for the first time as a mum on my own.

In any case, compared to many mums who don't have any support, I know I am extremely lucky. My friend Joely is a single mum who also had a Caesarean and after spending three days in hospital returned home alone and had to face four flights of stairs carrying her baby to her flat. To make matters worse the building was on a red route, which meant that even after she was able to drive again she was unable to park outside to get her little one out of the car or to unload groceries. Instead she had to park around the corner and struggle up the stairs with her baby in the car seat and her shopping bags. I've always admired Joely for the way she has brought up Téa on her own to be a well-mannered little girl but even more so since becoming a mum myself. She's a superwoman in my eyes.

For my own trip home I had booked a cab and luckily the driver was really friendly, helping me with all my luggage which had somehow tripled in size during my stay at the Portland. (And no, I hadn't stolen a dressing gown, towels or anything else from the hospital for that matter!) He had a right giggle at me as I spent ten minutes fumbling with Betsy's car seat, making sure it was all safe and secure and the straps were in the right place. I was slightly paranoid about the car seat as a friend told me they knew someone who had bought a second-hand one only to find it was broken when they put their newborn into it for the first time. You have to be so careful with buying things that are second-hand – in fact I've read you should never buy second-hand car seats, as crash damage doesn't always show. Luckily Betsy's seat was all working fine once I'd got the hang of it.

As we made our way to Hampstead the driver chatted away, telling me I had years of fun ahead if his experiences with his kids and grandkids were anything to go by. Despite his friendly conversation I barely lifted my head throughout the journey – even when one of my favourite songs, Take That's 'Back for Good', came on the radio – as I was so busy just staring at Betsy, her tiny hands safely covered by pristine white scratch mitts and her head kept warm with a tiny hat. I felt a flutter of butterflies in my stomach – a mixture of nerves and excitement – about our new life. She, of course, seemed slightly less excited and snoozed all the way.

As I sat in the back of the taxi it dawned on me that, despite the build-up over the last nine months and all the blogs and magazines I'd read, I was totally unprepared. I didn't have a clue what I was doing! What if I did it all wrong? What if Betsy didn't like me? Was it normal to feel this way? All sorts of crazy thoughts started whizzing through my mind. I guess it's because, unlike a new microwave or washing machine, your little bundle of joy doesn't come with an instruction manual (although now I was thinking about it, I was reminded that my last microwave ended with a big bang and a cloud of smoke! Now was probably not the time to dwell on that...).

The realisation that there was so much to learn was freaking me out – I hardly knew where to start. I wondered how my mum had coped back when she had me. I'm the youngest of three, so when I arrived she was out of hospital the following day to look after all three of us – my sister Jackie who was five, my brother Terry who was two, and me. My mum told me that by the time I came along she was a dab hand at the delivery process but hadn't been prepared for how tired she would feel with three little ones demanding her attention. My dad was working ridiculously long hours at Tilbury Docks in Essex to bring home the bacon because there was no paternity leave back in the 1970s, so mum looked after us on her own and would always make sure there was a good hearty meal waiting for my dad when he came home every evening. Women were made of strong stuff in those days. Lee would have a heart attack if he came home and I'd done so much as save him a couple of slices of my pizza – which I seemed to live on for the first few days of being at home. Mind you, if you can't hang up your oven gloves for a few weeks after giving birth, when can you?

As we got closer to home I did what we all tend to do when we have been away for a few days – I started making a mental shopping list of the basics I would need, such as fresh milk for a cup of tea and a packet of Custard Creams. I knew Lee had spent more time in the theatre than at home recently so we were bound to be low on everything. I asked the driver to pull over at my local shop so I could run in and grab what I needed. But then, as he drew up to the kerb, I looked over at Betsy and it hit me – I realised I couldn't just jump out and leave her. There was my precious bundle sat there – the last thing I was going to do was leave her with a complete stranger, however nice he was, while I popped to get a pint of milk. And after the palaver of strapping her chair in at the hospital I wasn't about to take her in with me either. I didn't realise it at the time, but this was going to become a regular occurrence over the next few weeks, with me arranging girlie nights out and then promptly cancelling them as I came to terms with the fact that my life wasn't the same any more. I couldn't just do what I wanted, when I wanted – I had Betsy to look after. And for now, at least, the tea and biscuits would just have to wait.

As we pulled up outside our flat my jaw dropped – the building was covered in scaffolding and there were workmen everywhere. This wasn't going to be fun! To make matters worse the driver spotted a couple of photographers waiting over the road – they must have been taking it in turns to watch my front door for the last week, which seemed pretty crazy – so I had to cover Betsy's car seat over before jumping out of the car and making a dash for it. The lovely driver helped me carry all my stuff into the flat and after saying our goodbyes I closed the door. Home at last.

Home Sweet Home

When we fall pregnant us ladies are genetically designed to nest, to prepare for when we bring our baby home so they're as comfortable as possible. We've all been there, right? Even if you don't realise you've been doing it, I'll bet you have, just a teensy bit. I painted the entire flat, bleached every surface multiple times – I couldn't get enough of the smell of bleach while I was pregnant – and for some slightly over-the-top reason decided we needed new lights which could be dimmed in every room. I went mad moving furniture around and throwing things out. Poor Lee, he lost half his wardrobe. Then you find yourself biting your other half's head off for sitting in the wrong chair and making the place look untidy (or is that just me?!). Yet despite playing out the moment I'd get to bring Betsy home over and over again in my head beforehand, I hadn't actually thought much further than walking through the front door.

I literally didn't know what to do once we were in the hallway so I walked through to the front room, placed the car seat containing Betsy right in the centre of the floor, and introduced her to the flat by saying, 'OK, this is where you live.' I sat on the sofa and lost a few more minutes staring at her. Or maybe it was an hour, who knows? I'm convinced you can travel forward in time by staring at a baby – where else would all those lost hours go? When I finally came back to the real world I took her on a guided tour showing her all the rooms in our flat, introducing her to the first-ever place she would call home.

Of course special attention was paid to her nursery, the room I'd spent the last few months decorating, making sure it was just right and hoping she'd have the same taste in wallpaper as I did. I kept her nursery fairly neutral, decorating it with red gingham cushions, a mobile and a big padded letter 'B' and in the end opting for an oatmeal-coloured wallpaper with gold bees on it. I had to talk Lee around at first as he thought it was a bit grown-up for the nursery but I persuaded him that it would be perfect for when she gets a bit older too so we'd get more use out of it (look at me being all thrifty!). I've also got classic black-and-white prints of movie stars such as Greta Garbo, Michael Caine and Faye Dunaway throughout the flat and wanted to keep the theme, so I bought two pictures of Shirley Temple for Betsy's nursery, including one in which she is holding a big swirly lollipop. I positioned it over the change table and for the first six months Betsy was transfixed by it every time I changed her nappy.

To complete the room there was a whole army of cuddly toys to greet Betsy, some with her name on to make her feel at home, as well as a few old favourites like Peter Rabbit and Mickey Mouse. There was one bear in particular that still takes pride of place which was a gift from Betsy's great-grandma, Lee's nan. I'm sure she won it at bingo, bless her. Unfortunately she passed away six weeks after Betsy was born without getting to meet her – she was ill in hospital before she died and sadly we weren't allowed to take Betsy to visit. I'll make sure the bear is kept in her keepsake box for when she is older and I know it'll be something she'll treasure.

I'm guessing you get the picture that the nursery couldn't have been more ready for its new resident? We all know babies aren't supposed to smile when they are newborn but I'm pretty sure Betsy gave me a little smile to let me know she approved.

At 11.30 pm Lee finally joined us after his rehearsal at the theatre, and I'll never forget his face as he walked in. He burst through the door like he'd just scooped the

Euro Millions jackpot! He dashed right over to Betsy who was fast asleep in her Moses basket, then came over to me and said, 'Hello, Mum.' For a moment I sat there confused, expecting his mum to walk into the room – before registering what he meant. It seemed really weird being called mum and I felt quite emotional. It was a new nametag I was going to have to get used to. I've been called many, many things over the years, but this was the first time I'd been called 'mum' and I really liked it. We both just sat there mesmerised by our new addition for ages, and when we did talk it was at a whisper so we didn't wake her. Every so often she'd move and we'd look back at each other, our faces beaming with pride. I couldn't believe we'd created something so amazing.

We tucked into pizza – despite the freezer being stocked full with meals I'd prepared while I was pregnant – and drank copious amounts of tea while watching *Gavin and Stacey* on DVD. I'd ordered a few DVD box sets of some of the series we'd missed while we'd been performing in shows so we'd have plenty to keep us entertained while spending cosy evenings in with our new daughter. I remember feeling really silly about getting so emotional when Nessa told Smithy she was pregnant with his baby, something I would have never done before. I guess becoming a mum had unlocked a mushy side to me. It's something that seems to happen to a lot of new parents – I have one friend who would cry if she heard a particular song on the radio and another who would only watch *The X Factor* alone so she could blub in private without feeling embarrassed.

We eventually went to bed at 1 am, both Lee and I unable to keep our eyes open any longer. Lee would be working so we'd decided that I would sleep with Betsy in her nursery for the foreseeable future to allow us to both get enough sleep. As we said goodnight, there was a moment when I wondered whether Lee had listened to anything I had relayed to him from my antenatal classes. I'm sure dads suffer from 'baby brain' too. He asked me whether he should set an alarm for 7 am in the morning because that's what time babies wake up! I laughed my head off although I could have quite easily clocked him one too. He went on to explain that he thought it was just while we were in hospital that Betsy would wake up so often in the night. Little did he know the sleep deprivation that lay ahead.

First Night at Home

After visiting many of my friends with newborns over the past few years I was prepared for the chaos and lack of sleep that comes with having a new baby. I'd heard all sorts of stories from friends about them being too worried to sleep for fear of their baby choking or stopping breathing, but to be completely honest I think I was so exhausted that as soon as my head hit the pillow I was out like a light! Luckily Betsy slept well too, only waking to be fed every couple of hours or so. It was really weird at first sitting there feeding Betsy, firstly because I was still trying to master the art of breastfeeding and spent ages trying to get Betsy to latch on to my nipple properly and, secondly, knowing that whilst I was doing this pretty much everyone else in the world (maybe a slight exaggeration) was fast asleep. It was so quiet in the flat I could hear every creak, and despite having Betsy in my arms I couldn't help but feel slightly lonely. I took a look on Twitter to see if anyone else was awake at such a ridiculous hour and was surprised to see how many people were on it, complaining about not being able to sleep. I tweeted to say I was up feeding Betsy and within seconds I'd had loads of replies from mums saying they were doing the same. It felt good to know that I wasn't alone and that there was a whole army of mothers out there feeding their little ones in the dead of night. Some mums also offered me advice on how to stay awake by downloading games to my mobile or by having a flask containing a nice hot drink next to the bed.

I'd positioned Betsy's Moses basket right next to my side of the bed so I could see her. When she did occasionally wake up and cry I'd go through the mental checklist. Does she have a dirty nappy? Is she hungry? Has she had enough sleep? It was always one of these options. Some of my mates had told me they could actually tell what was wrong by the tone of their baby's cry but to be honest it all sounded the same to me in the early days.

When I woke up the following morning I lay there for a while and it was only when I rolled over and spotted the empty Moses basket next to me that it dawned on me that I was home with Betsy. Then I heard Lee's voice coming from the kitchen. I thought he was on the phone to his mum at first but when I walked in he was washing Betsy's face with tiny cotton wool balls and telling her everything he was doing. It was a really lovely sight to wake up to. I'd told Lee it was important to talk as much as possible to Betsy as it really helps to develop a baby's brain; he had felt really silly for the first few days but had soon got the hang of it. I still chat away constantly to Betsy now whether she's listening or not (and even when she's asleep).

I must look like a madwoman at times when I'm out and about constantly narrating my actions.

Everything Is OK

Luckily I had Lee's help in getting Betsy ready and into another gorgeous little outfit so I could grab a quick shower, as mid-morning we received an unannounced visit from a midwife. They do that so they can see how you are really coping and not be fooled by any extra effort that has been made for their visit (a bit like a mystery shopper, although instead of rating service or food they're rating your ability as a mum – scary!). Little did she know that if she'd turned up an hour earlier, she'd have caught me knee-deep in poo. She weighed Betsy, checked my stitches, and told us we were doing nicely all round. It was such a relief to hear that everything was fine with Betsy, because as the midwife was doing her checks I'm sure I held my breath a few times. She also told me that I seemed to be coping well, which made me grow an inch. It's like being told you're a star pupil by the headmaster. I know midwives do a brilliant job and are there to help but I couldn't help but feel like I was being put to the test – new mummy paranoia, I guess!

Rub-a-Dub-Dub

That afternoon while Lee was at work I decided I would give Betsy a bath as Lee had given her her first dip while we were in hospital (to this day he still proudly tells Betsy 'Daddy gave you your first bath!') and she seemed to really enjoy it. I told myself there was nothing to worry about as I had everything I could possibly need laid out ready but it wasn't long before I freaked out. I'd bought a special support to go into a bath for Betsy to lie on but somehow the bath looked huge with it in and bending down over it after having a Caesarean didn't seem like the best idea. I couldn't work out how I was going to safely lean over the side and wash her without popping my stitches or putting my back out.

Within minutes I was on the phone to my number-one support-team member, my mum, who told me she'd bathed my brother, sister and I in the kitchen sink for the first couple of months and we turned out all right. I made an instant decision that the family tradition would continue and for the first few months Betsy would take her daily plunge in the sink, until such time as she was big enough for the proper bath and my scar had healed enough for me to feel confident lifting her in and out and bending over. Of course it helps that both Lee and I are borderline OCD when it comes to housework so our sink is always clean and free of dishes!

Betsy's first dip in the sink was really special. I'd wrapped towels around the edge so that it was padded if Betsy's head touched it and after testing the temperature three or four times, in case the thermometer was wrong, I carefully lowered her into the water. I waited for a response and was so pleased when she stared at me with wide eyes and gave a little wriggle. There wasn't a hint of her being upset, which made me smile because I'm told I often used to scream the house down at bath time (thankfully that's one thing I've grown out of over the years...).

Despite having all the lotions and potions that exist for babies I decided to bath her in plain water for at least the first couple of weeks as the last thing I wanted was to irritate Betsy's precious skin. Once I'd dried her gently and fairly quickly – I didn't want her to tinkle everywhere – I did put a tiny bit of Burt's Bees baby cream over her and she smelled lovely. Her bottom and legs were so cute – I now understand why people say the phrase 'as smooth as a baby's bottom'.

A word from my Twitter followers

Louise, mum to a three-month-old daughter

After a difficult labour that eventually led to a C-section, I was finally allowed home and felt overwhelmed by the whole experience. Nothing I'd read prepared me for being alone for the first time with my baby. As soon as I walked through the door I felt strange and within minutes of sitting down it hit me that I was now without the help or advice of the midwives who'd been looking after me. When Summer began to cry I started to panic until it dawned on me that she may need her nappy changing. Of course when I attended to it, she immediately stopped crying. I found the first two weeks very emotional and tiring and although I had my boyfriend at home most of the time I had to learn to do everything on my own. Things are now wonderful: Summer is a beautiful three-month-old and is sleeping through most of the night.

Maxine, mum to five-month-old twin girls

My girls were born eleven weeks early as my kidneys and liver had started to fail so I needed to deliver them for the sake of my health. Holly and Emily were kept in the neonatal intensive care unit for nine weeks before they were able to leave the hospital. We couldn't wait to get them home and there were occasions when it felt like the day would never come. We didn't feel like real parents as we could only spend the daytime with our girls before we'd have to leave them and go home at night. It was wonderful to finally have them home – although the first night we only got one hour's sleep!

Louise, mum to a seven-month-old son

I stayed in the hospital for two nights, as I couldn't get my son to latch on properly. I slept for about twenty minutes the first night, and one hour the second. Emotional and exhausted, the last thing I needed was the breastfeeding woman getting me to try out everything from the rugby position to the on-the-bed-Miranda-Kerr pose! In the end I was allowed home after expressing, which took forever. Walking into my home, which had been decorated with balloons and flowers by my sister and mum, I took photos of my husband holding the car seat with our sleeping little boy, Harry. It was immense, exciting and I felt like a real woman with a responsibility. A huge one.

Jessica, mum to a three-year-old daughter and a six-year-old son

My daughter was due on Boxing Day. I probably jinxed myself from the moment I found out I was pregnant by always saying how it would be just my luck to be in labour on Christmas Day – and of course I was! Labour started on Christmas Eve and, even though I tried to ignore the initial signs, I was in full labour on Christmas morning. I managed to stay at home with my son, who was then three, to open his presents before leaving for the hospital. Our baby daughter, Ava was born three minutes before midday and shortly after we were offered a hospital Christmas lunch – urgh! Instead we left hospital at 3 pm, put the turkey in the oven as soon as we got home and the whole family had a late Christmas dinner.

Alison, mum to a two-year-old son

My son Jack came out fist-first like Superman when he was born. We were allowed home the following day and all seemed well. When he became unsettled and wouldn't feed I called the midwife who came round to check on him. She called an ambulance straight away and told me he had an infection. At Manchester Children's Hospital he underwent tests and the results showed that Jack had meningitis and septicemia brought on by Group B Strep – an infection I had unknowingly passed on to him during the birth. He also had bleeding on the brain and we were told that if he survived Jack would likely have significant brain damage. Two and a half years on, Jack is absolutely perfect. Miraculously he beat all the infections, was out of hospital after two weeks and has had no signs of any developmental problems at all so far.

Lizzy, mum to a four-month-old daughter

Our daughter Grace had always loved bath time from the very first one I gave her in hospital up until she was age eight weeks, when she suddenly started screaming and crying when we took her out of the bath right up until she had finished her bedtime bottle. I researched the problem and tried various things like splitting her last bottle in case she was too hungry and putting her towel on the radiator in case it was making her cold when I got her out. In the end I received some advice on a forum from a lady who suggested that perhaps Grace loves her bath so much that she simply hates getting out! I'd never considered that could be the case, so I decided to make getting out of the bath fun. I sing to her when she is in the bath so I made sure I carried on singing to her and playing while I took her out. It's worked!

Chapter 3

I Think We're Alone Now

I remember reading somewhere when I was pregnant that you can spot a first-time mum a mile off, as she'll be the one struggling to do everything on her own – while the second timers upwards will be directing an army of helpers from their bed while they catch up on some sleep! That's definitely true. I wanted to turn down all offers of assistance at first because I thought that if we accepted them, we'd be admitting that we couldn't cope. A mother's guilt is a powerful thing, and something I was only just starting to get my head around. Luckily, some of my mates who have little ones pretty quickly pointed out that we'd be absolutely mad not to accept help – otherwise I think I would have reached breaking point before I admitted I could do with a hand. To add to my luck, Betsy's grandparents were chomping at the bit to muck in.

I didn't realise at the time, but I certainly couldn't have got through the first few weeks without my mum and dad. They stayed with us at the flat the first week we were back and were such a huge help. My dad went off to do a big shop for me, bless him (to this day I can still picture him scratching his head and looking bemused in the nappy aisle), while my mum took care of the chores around the house – she was like a woman possessed in my flowery Marigolds – stopping only to give Betsy plenty of cuddles.

I became much closer to my mum during that week. I guess we now had motherhood in common, and I think you can only really appreciate everything your parents did for you when you're in that situation yourself. I was suddenly hit by this huge wave of gratitude for everything she went through and sacrificed for me, my brother and sister.

Funnily enough, this felt like one of the first times in my adult life that I really needed my mum, which I think made a nice change for her. I've always been pretty self-sufficient; I left school and got a job straight away, and although my mum has always tried to help me over the years I've just got on with things on my own. So I'm certain she got as much out of that week as I did. She had plenty of good advice on the best way to do things, which I took on board for the most part, and thankfully she struck the perfect balance between offering me her words of wisdom and letting me learn for myself. I've always had a good relationship with my mum so it was easy to tell her if I felt she was taking over a bit, but that was rarely the case.

It was such a relief for us all to come together so well, as I have friends who felt their parents or in-laws criticised them or undermined their early parenting skills. One mate told me that her mum would hardly talk to her but instead direct everything at the baby, saying things like, 'Oh Billy, are your feet cold, do you think you need some socks on?' With the typical sensitivity of a first-time parent my friend took it as criticism and would feel anger bubbling up inside her – she'd have to bite her tongue to stop herself from shouting, 'He's fine but if it makes you happy then you go upstairs and get him some socks!' Can you imagine?!

Lee's family were great too and would pop over at the drop of a hat if we needed anything. I can laugh now but I remember watching the film *Monster-in-Law* starring Jennifer Lopez and sitting in horror as the mother-in-law-to-be did everything she could to split up her son and Jennifer Lopez's character. I was single at the time and seriously prayed that the man I ended up with didn't have a mother like her. It could have happened! I have a friend who had been busy planning her wedding during pregnancy and the early stages of motherhood, but when her mother-in-law began criticising her on how she was caring for her baby things turned sour, firstly between them and then with her partner, as she felt he wasn't backing her up. Not only was the wedding cancelled just a few months before it was due to take place – which is such a shame in itself – but the couple actually separated soon afterwards. I can't imagine what it would feel like to have that kind of stress on top of everything else you have to contend with as a new mum.

On Our Own

After a week of having amazing support at home the time felt right for the three of us to go it alone. Betsy was twelve days old and was already looking far more robust than when she was born. And besides, my mum would always be on the other end of the phone or on Skype if I needed advice or just a sympathetic ear. Despite it feeling like the right thing to do, I still experienced a wave of sadness as Lee, Betsy and I stood on the doorstep to wave my mum and dad goodbye. It took a while to get used to the flat being so quiet but as the three of us snuggled up together on the sofa to watch yet more *Gavin and Stacey* on DVD it felt wonderful.

The next few days didn't feel quite so wonderful as I came to terms with the building work that was taking place on my doorstep. The place was a mess and we were surrounded by scaffolding as workmen re-pointed the building and took out all the window frames to replace them. No one had informed me that it was going to take place but there was nothing I could do about it. The building work created a huge amount of dirt and brick dust, which was hardly conducive to keeping my precious baby clean and safe! Betsy looked so tiny and fragile that the last thing I wanted was to take her in and out of the flat via a building site, so we were basically housebound.

Looking back, being surrounded by scaffolding and builders really affected my mood in these early weeks – especially after spending such an amazing first few days being looked after by the nurses at the Portland. There was a Portaloo outside my living-room window where the workmen would do their business so I had no option but to keep the curtains drawn the whole time. They would stand in my garden – the garden that I should have been sat in with Betsy in the hammock I'd bought especially – and smoke like chimneys before throwing the cigarette ends on the grass. Looking back now I should have ordered a catapult online and had some fun but at the time I felt very vulnerable. I had to keep moving rooms each day depending on where they were painting the window frames because the fumes were overpowering, so we'd usually spend the entire day holed up in the same room and even then I couldn't open the window for some fresh air because all we would have got was more fumes and dust. I'd cheer myself up by watching Peter Andre's show (you've got to love a bit of Pete!) which I'd recorded over the last few weeks, but there were times when I felt so frustrated and miserable I'd sit cuddling Betsy and cry. I had so wanted this to be a time that was full of happy memories and it was being spoilt.

Luckily we had visitors pretty much each day so they would soon cheer me up if I was feeling a bit down. Betsy was the centre of attention of course but I was happy to hand her over and do normal things like making a cup of tea and some sandwiches.

Lee and I had worked out a code for if/when visitors had outstayed their welcome and we needed some peace. One of us would say to the other that we had other guests coming to visit soon and this would be a cue to turf people out. This master plan should have been ideal for when a couple of Lee's friends came round to meet Betsy when she was three weeks old. The only slight flaw was that Lee has a terrible memory. Having waited on them with tea and biscuits all morning I was looking forward to a quiet afternoon once Lee had left for the theatre to do the afternoon matinee. As Lee grabbed his coat I mentioned my friend Sam would be round at one o'clock, thinking he'd step into action and invite his friends to leave with him. But oh no! Instead he grumbled that I hadn't told him Sam was coming and he wished he didn't have to work so he could be there too. I couldn't believe it! As he went off to work his friends told me they wouldn't stay too much longer but they were really enjoying having such a relaxing day. I felt like screaming, but of course I bit my lip and in true Brit style put the kettle on. Before I'd got as far as making another brew one of them said, 'I know it's a bit cheeky but I really fancy a glass of white wine.' A bottle later they were still curled up on my sofa. I eventually got rid of them at 6 pm – a whole nine hours after they had arrived when I should have been recuperating instead. I still kick myself for not saying something – they would hardly have taken offence if I'd said I was tired and needed to rest – but I guess it's a Brit thing to suffer in silence while quietly going mad inside.

Venturing Out

Betsy was six weeks old when I finally plucked up the courage to take her to the high street in her buggy on my own. Up until then the only time I had been out of the flat with her was to go to a photo shoot and I had my mate Tamara with me to help me look after Betsy and get her in and out of a cab. I know that's quite late to venture out – my mate Sam took her baby April to Brent Cross shopping centre when she was just two days old and I have friends who've been on long-haul flights with their babies in the first month. I had been apprehensive about taking Betsy out with all the work that was taking place outside the flat but now she had put on more weight, I began to feel more comfortable with my ability to look after her. As my confidence grew, so did my cabin fever, so eventually it came time to take on the outside world.

Lee was at work that afternoon and I decided I needed a bit of moral support, so I announced on Twitter that today was my first day out and I was feeling a little nervous. It was the best thing I could have done: the response I got from my followers was amazing. Not only did I get many lovely messages of encouragement, with people saying I should enjoy every minute, but also great advice on what I should remember to take with me (most of which I'd forgotten, of course). After yet another last-minute nappy change – babies sure have good timing – I'd almost given up for the day, but I eventually made it out the door.

It was a gorgeous sunny afternoon as Betsy and I hit Hampstead High Street. It just feels great to be out with your little one for the first time, a strange mix of absolute stand-tall, chest-out pride and uneasiness at having to push a pram around. You feel like you should have L-plates on and that everyone's staring at you, but then you look up and notice there's a hundred other mums with prams everywhere, taking it all in their stride, so I tried, as my tweeters quite rightly advised, to just enjoy every minute.

Every time I looked down to see my precious cargo wrapped up snugly, occasionally opening her eyes to take in the view, it made me beam with pride and my heart would melt just a little bit more. I'm sure this is the way every new parent feels but I just kept thinking she was the most beautiful baby in the world! All that gazing at her adoringly must really take it out of you though, as after only a couple of minutes I felt absolutely exhausted. No one warns you about how much stuff you have to lug around with a baby, and pushing all of that in a big pram around the hilly streets of Hampstead ain't easy, especially when you suffer from a bad back as I do. I was surprised as I'm quite fit and had carried on exercising until a month before I had Betsy, but I guess you can't underestimate how much having a baby and then caring for one takes it out of you. I suddenly realised why I always saw so many mums in Starbucks – they weren't necessarily socialising, they were having a pit-stop! Well, I'm a mum now and if you can't beat 'em, join 'em, I say, so I pulled in for a well-earned break in the shape of a soya latte and a blueberry muffin.

It's weird as I'd never paid that much attention to other mums before but now I couldn't help but watch out of the corner of my eye to see how they did things. I probably looked really rude as I watched mums cuddle, feed and entertain their babies but this was almost like a real-life parenting class for me, far better than messing around with the plastic doll in my antenatal classes. After that I popped into Boots to browse the baby section. I didn't need anything, but it felt good to walk around the aisles with a pram asking Betsy if she wanted this or that. She was far away in the land of nod of course, so I probably looked like a right nutter, but even a gurgle or a slight movement was a seal of approval.

Disappointingly I'd had to leave my handbag at home – and anyone who knows me will realise how hard that was for me as I love my handbags. But I just couldn't work out a safe place to carry it on the pram. After checking with my tweeters and my mummy friends again it became clear that it would have to be out with my lovely handbags and in with a dedicated pocket in the change bag from now on. This actually horrified me. Nappies and sleepless nights I could handle, but no one had warned me about this! I remember emptying my Chloe bag one day to see how many of the baby essentials I could fit inside it in the hope of rocking a glam-mum look, but alas it didn't work. It's designed to hold a purse and some mascara, not nappies, wipes and the other million baby essentials you need to hand.

Going out with Betsy for the first time had been a lovely learning curve. My first grocery shopping trip with her in tow? Not so much. In fact, it was an absolute nightmare. I'd just popped into Tesco to buy a few essential items, but on autopilot filled my basket with plenty of things I didn't really need – two-for-one conditioners, cereal, dishwasher tablets, washing powder and so on. It wasn't until I reached the checkout and started packing my bags that I realised I wasn't going to be able to get it all home. What prams actually need are trailers of some kind, rather than a small shelf underneath, which in my case was already full with a couple of things I'd bought earlier. I felt so embarrassed as I struggled with the rest of my shopping, most of which ended up in the bassinet with Betsy. I was conscious of looking like such a novice mum as I walked out of the shop, Betsy wedged between a box of cornflakes and some PG Tips. That same evening I signed up to do my shopping online for the first time, which was nothing short of a revelation – I honestly believe online supermarket shopping must have been invented by a mum who had experienced the same nightmare shopping trip as I had.

Crying in Public

The first time Betsy cried in public will be etched on my mind forever! I'd been expecting (and dreading) it but even so, when it happened in a queue in my local post office it was absolutely horrendous. I'd been waiting in line for ages when Betsy started to grizzle. I tried to shush her but it seemed to make her worse and, before I knew it, the cry had escalated into a full-on scream. I'm used to being looked at in public but this was different. I felt as if everyone's eyes were burning through me, which made me feel really self-conscious. My whole body began to burn up and I started sweating. It's a horrible feeling because the last thing I want is for my baby to be upset – like any mum her comfort and happiness is the most important thing in the world to me – but at the same time I was willing her to stop simply because I was feeling a bit embarrassed. Is that normal? I hope so!

I did everything I could to calm Betsy down but she just kept going at the top of her voice all the way through the queue, up to the counter and while I was being served. Thankfully the cashier was understanding and after giving me a sympathetic smile told me to take my time as I fumbled around in my bag desperately trying to find my purse. I managed to post my parcel and escape from the furnace of the post office to the coolness of outside. Then, right on cue, as we began to walk up the high street she stopped – typical. At just a couple of months old it seems my little girl doesn't have the patience for queuing.

Of course feeling embarrassed doesn't stop it happening and you do get used to it, but the first time is definitely the worst. In hindsight the people who did look over were probably just being inquisitive or even not looking at us in reality. We've all stood in a queue behind a crying baby and just taken a cursory glance and then forgotten about it. But that doesn't stop you feeling like you're in the centre of a spotlit stage when it's your baby who's doing the crying!

Baby Blues

I was prepared to experience an array of emotions after Betsy arrived, because I had friends who had not only told me about the highs they experienced soon after giving birth but had also confided in me as they were going through the tougher times. A couple of them were frustrated that they didn't have enough time for themselves; one friend told me that her husband was uncharacteristically jealous and she thought it was because he was feeling pushed out by their new baby; while another did nothing but worry about whether she was being a good mum or not.

I experienced a fabulous high for the few days after Betsy arrived. I remember Dannii Minogue saying she wished she could have bottled how she felt soon after becoming a mum to her son Ethan, as she'd make a fortune selling it. I know what she meant as it is such a wonderful feeling of contentment mixed with a belief that you are capable of achieving anything. But as the saying goes, 'What goes up must come down,' and once the high had worn off I felt an overwhelming sense of responsibility. I'd only had to take care of myself before and now I had a little person who was solely dependent on Lee and me to take care of her. Of course my own needs took a backseat as a result – which meant painting my nails, shaving my legs, popping out on the spur of the moment and catching up with friends became a thing of the past. It wasn't long before frustration crept in as I felt like I was always playing catch-up, and on the rare occasion I sat down with a cup of tea I'd have endless 'to-do' lists running through my head.

Despite my frustrations I managed to keep on top of things for a while but that all changed when Betsy reached three weeks old and I got hit hard by the baby blues.

Despite having friends who have suffered from depression after giving birth I didn't put two and two together to realise that was what I was experiencing – all I knew was I felt miserable and agitated. To make matters worse, Betsy went from being content to lie in her Moses basket or on a play mat to constantly crying unless I was holding her. This made things really difficult because I'd automatically pick her up to comfort her but then find I was unable to get anything done. Even a trip to the loo would mean spending a penny with Betsy's cry ringing in my ears.

I didn't have a clue what to do and the friends I asked gave me conflicting advice. One told me to hold her close whenever she cried to reassure her because she was so young, while another friend, who doesn't have any children, told me I was making a rod for my own back by picking her up every time she cried and I should leave her to cry it out. I found it very confusing and upsetting. As any mother will know, it's nigh on impossible to leave your baby crying when all it takes is a cuddle for them to stop.

Betsy's crying gradually calmed down but from this point until Betsy was three months old I felt weird. Really weird. I still had plenty of happy days with Betsy – such as the afternoon I'd taken her round Hampstead High Street – but as time went on there was an underlying sense that something was dragging me down. I felt dazed, as if I'd survived three rounds with Mike Tyson, and that was coupled with mild self-loathing where I just couldn't please myself and certainly didn't feel in the least bit attractive. I'd look in the mirror and staring back at me was Cruella De Vil. No matter how much of an effort I made with my appearance, I felt like a mess. Lee was great and constantly paid me compliments – even when I asked him whether I looked the same as I did pre-pregnancy for the hundredth time he would still raise a smile and tell me I looked even better. But I found it hard not having as much time for myself as I used to. My once-luxurious baths and showers became more of a military operation – a quick dip and I was out. And let's just say my lady garden ended up looking more like Hampstead Heath than a prize-winning entry at the Chelsea Flower Show.

One way or another I felt like my whole life changed overnight – I went from being a strong, smart, independent woman who does what she likes when she likes to suddenly not being in control at all any more. It was a shock to the system.

Of course whenever I saw any friends and family they'd offer the standard comments and compliments that seem almost obligatory when you see someone soon after they've given birth, such as 'You look great!' and 'You wouldn't know you've just had a baby!' But the truth is no one is going to tell you that you look like crap, and no matter what anyone tells you it's how you feel that counts – and I often felt awful. The only way I can describe it is if you imagine PMT times 100. You can find yourself at a set of traffic lights with tears in your eyes wondering what the hell's wrong with you, and then you get stressed out as you can't figure out why you're feeling that way.

I didn't tell anyone how I was feeling for a long time because I didn't want to speak about it or, I suppose, admit it to myself. I've always been very good at putting on a front to hide my true feelings when I'm down; it's in my nature and I suppose it comes with the territory of being in the public eye. I have to be very careful who I reveal any personal details to as I've had private stuff written in the papers about me in the past. I also wasn't entirely sure exactly how I was feeling – it seemed to change from one minute to the next – so I decided not to discuss it with my friends or family. Of course I'd act as gracious as I could when I received a compliment but I'd often have been far happier hidden under my duvet where I didn't have to face anyone.

As the saying goes, hindsight is 20/20 and looking back at how I felt I was definitely in the grips of a bout of the baby blues. Since I realised what happened and have started to open up and talk about it, a few of my friends and colleagues have told me they also suffered from either depression or the baby blues and they too didn't realise what was going on until they came out the other side.

The crazy thing is that having a baby should be a happy occasion and up until the point where the baby blues hit me I had been enjoying every minute. Then all of a sudden when everything isn't quite so rosy you start to beat yourself up over the fact you are feeling down when you have been blessed with a gorgeous baby. The imbalance of hormones that mothers have to deal with after birth is absolutely crazy and something I don't think any of us truly expect the first time round. I certainly didn't. I remember reading that postnatal depression affects one in ten women (although it could be higher due to women not seeking help) and most women experience some degree of baby blues, whether it be an outpouring of emotions on day three of becoming a mum that passes within a few hours or something that sticks around longer and is much harder to shake.

I've come to realise that there are definitely varying degrees of depression or baby blues and I got away quite lightly in relation to what some women go through. I remember reading an interesting interview with Katie Price where she really opened up about the postnatal depression she experienced after giving birth to her second son, Junior. She spoke about how she had trouble bonding with him and was admitted to the Priory where they put her on antidepressants. Gwyneth Paltrow has also been open about her struggles with PND. She had experienced all the highs of becoming a mum when she had Apple but when she gave birth to Moses she described it as feeling like she couldn't access her heart or her emotions and as a result felt like a terrible mother. I just can't imagine what that would feel like. It must be such an awful feeling that absolutely tears you apart because deep down you know this little person is dependent on you and needs your love. I think it's a really good thing for people who are in the public eye to speak out about the tough times they have been through because it brings it into the press and will help others to be more open about how they are feeling.

Luckily the internet is an amazing source of advice and support these days. I met a mum quite recently through a campaign I was working on who suffered from terrible postnatal depression. Having now come out of the other side of it, she has started writing a blog about her experiences so that other mothers can identify with what she went through and not feel alone. I would have really benefited from reading something like that while I was experiencing the baby blues as I'm sure it would have helped me to realise why I was feeling the way I was.

My negative feelings gradually subsided on their own but it definitely took a good year for me to feel normal again. Many women aren't so lucky – especially those who are suffering from full-scale postnatal depression rather than just a milder dose of 'baby blues' – and it's not until they seek help that they can start moving towards feeling themselves once more. It's so important for mums experiencing any kind of change in emotions as a result of pregnancy to realise they are not alone and there are other mums out there having similar thoughts, no matter how bad they are. A fully trained professional will help you without making judgement.

Smile, Baby

Despite the bumpy road I experienced, I still have some wonderful memories of the early weeks at home with Betsy. One in particular makes me teary every time I think of it. There's nothing like seeing your baby smile for the first time and Betsy was six weeks old when she flashed me her first real smile. I say 'real' because I lost count of the number of times I thought Betsy was smiling before that – her timing was impeccable but, as everyone tells you, before that age it's probably just wind.

There was no mistaking the first real time, though. I was at home making some of the sounds I do during a vocal warm-up, which is something you do each night before going on stage when appearing in a musical. I guess I do it out of habit now instead of whistling or humming. I made a silly high-pitched noise and hey presto, she smiled – and her whole face and eyes lit up too! I called my mum in from the kitchen to see it, and when I made the noise for a second time Betsy smiled again. I actually got quite emotional because it was the first kind of real communication we'd had; the first time she'd properly reacted to something I'd done or said. Despite my best efforts of dancing, singing and even high kicks, everything before that had been a one-way street so it felt great to get something back.

Needless to say Lee was over the moon when I told him our little girl had smiled and he couldn't wait for her to wake up the next morning so he could make 'the' noise himself (which of course he does in his vocal warm-ups too), and get his very own smile. We wore that noise out over the next couple of weeks – our poor neighbours must have thought we had gone mad. Not wanting the smiles to end we went on to pretend there was an aeroplane flying overhead – that went down a treat and her smile got even cheesier. I must have hundreds of photos of Betsy smiling, wearing different outfits and shot from different angles. It's pretty much the same photo to be fair but I can't bring myself to delete even one of them as I'll never get that time back again.

A word from my Twitter followers

Laura, mum to a five-month-old son

The first five months of my pregnancy were the most challenging and difficult months of my life and I ended up having therapy. I was terrified it would get even worse after my son was born as PND is so common. But as I had dealt with all my concerns so thoroughly while I was pregnant, I – we – are now the happiest EVER!

Nicola, mum to a three-year-old son

I was a week overdue with my son and was so excited about giving birth. I went into labour but we found out he was breech so I had to have a C-section. I was devastated, as it felt like one minute I was pregnant and the next I was handed a baby. I found it really hard to bond with my son and suffered with baby blues as a result.

Lisa, mum to a fourteen-year-old, ten-year-old, six-year-old and two-year-old

I'm a mum of four and suffered from baby blues with my first for what were undoubtedly the worst four weeks of my life. She was the only baby not to be placed straight on me for 'skin-to-skin' contact at birth and I always wonder if that contributed to the blues. I felt like a robot on autopilot feeding (by bottle), changing and dressing her. It got so bad that I thought I might hurt my baby so I left home and checked myself into a B&B. After five days I returned home and slowly began to bond with my daughter. I love her now but we don't share the same close tie that I have with my other three children.

Michelle, mum to a six-year-old daughter

I suffered with terrible postnatal depression while I was pregnant with my daughter and it didn't go away until she was two! Despite crying at anything and everything, I didn't tell anyone about it and didn't even admit to myself that there was something wrong. I don't think returning to full-time work when my daughter was just four months old helped. It wasn't until I started to take my daughter to a mother-and-toddler group and made a friend that I began smiling again.

Aimee, mum to a four-month-old daughter

A friend of mine tragically committed suicide while she was suffering from postnatal depression. So when I was pregnant I asked my close friends, family and husband to be vigilant and not to worry about offending me if they thought I was acting strange or not coping. It's important that those around you are aware of postnatal depression so they can spot it if you are unlucky to suffer from it.

Kate, mum of five

I have five kids now, aging from seventeen down to five. I suffered badly with depression after the births of my first two and battled not to let it get me with the others! I was only seventeen when I had my first, which I feel was one of the main problems. There were times when I almost felt like I hated the babies but it got better and I love them so much now.

Brenda, mum to a seven-year-old son

I had been warned about the third-day 'baby blues'. I woke up three days after giving birth with tender boobs but nothing major. My midwife commented on how cheery I was and couldn't believe I was showered, war paint on, with a clean, fed, dry baby in my arms. I silently and smugly congratulated myself on escaping the baby blues. By midday, my husband found me in a heap on the bedroom floor in floods of tears. The reason for my meltdown? I had inserted my son's birthday into my diary and spelled his name wrong. Terrible mother! My hubby insisted I take a nap but I couldn't bear the sound of my son crying so I went downstairs and came face to face with my mother-in-law who told me to pull myself together. The made-up, competent new mum from earlier had turned into a blotchy, puffy-faced mess. Later that evening while feeding my son, I was plotting to leave my husband as I had decided that I LOATHED him with a passion. I had every last detail worked out down to how often he would have contact with the baby. As I climbed the stairs back to bed, I was re-married and deliberating the etiquette for divorced parents at my son's imagined wedding. The next day I felt back to normal. Moral of the story: beware of the baby blues!

Chapter 4

What to Do for the Breast

'Breast is best' is a phrase mums-to-be can't escape. There are countless articles in magazines and newspapers promoting breastfeeding, TV shows dedicated to it and posters and leaflets on the subject all over the hospital when you attend regular check-ups throughout your pregnancy. There's no denying that breastfeeding comes with a whole heap of benefits – for example, it helps to form a stronger mother-and-baby bond, it boosts the baby's immune system and it reduces the likelihood of nappy rash. It is of course the cheaper feeding option, plus it means you don't have to lug around loads of bottles and sterilising equipment, which I wasn't looking forward to with my bad back. For a mum it reduces her risk of breast cancer and comes with a need to eat an extra 500 calories a day – a real bonus! Let's face it girls, who's going to complain about needing to tuck away more food than usual?! These are just a few of the many benefits I became aware of while reading through the chapters dedicated to the topic in my mountain of pregnancy books.

On paper, breastfeeding was definitely for me but from hearing some of my mates' experiences I knew it wasn't always that easy. I had a friend who desperately wanted to breastfeed her son but had a really tough time and wasn't able to get her baby to latch on from the word go. She suggested I keep an open mind. Like a lot of first-time mums who haven't got friends or family who have experienced difficulty, she had thought it would be straightforward – get her boob out, put her nipple in the baby's mouth and sit back and watch all gooey-eyed as her little one grew up fit and strong. She hadn't for one second considered that she might struggle or, worse still, not be able to breastfeed altogether. When she realised she would have to formula-feed she was really hard on herself. In fact she took it so badly that she ended up suffering terribly from baby blues. Thankfully she did exactly the right thing by seeking help and came to realise she was not alone – lots of women go through similar experiences.

To me it feels like the complications you can face while breastfeeding are the same as the pain you can experience during labour – it's as if no one wants to pre-warn you about them and it's all on a need-to-know basis. Which is fine for the lucky mums who breeze through childbirth and breastfeeding but not so good for those who don't.

On the other hand a couple of my mates were breastfeeding at the time I was pregnant and loving it. They couldn't speak more highly of their experience and loved how it made them feel so close to their babies. With a bit of juggling and expressing, their partners would take care of some feeds so they could catch up on some much-needed rest. Their initial wariness of feeding in public went out the window as soon as they perfected their latch-on techniques and within the first couple of weeks they were able to feed quite discreetly. My friends' experiences made me more determined than ever that I wanted to give it a go and they very kindly offered their services in the early days if I had any worries or questions. I was gathering my own personal breastfeeding squad.

One thing my mates didn't have to worry about which I had to take into consideration, though, was what I'd do when it came to feeding Betsy while out in public. I agree that it's the most natural thing in the world and mums should be able to do it anywhere. I love to see mums feeding their babies while out and about, and in fact before falling pregnant I had felt envious whenever I saw a mum enjoying that special connection. But most mums are able to find a quiet corner somewhere or breastfeed discreetly without so much as a second glance. I, on the other hand, spend most of the time outside my flat either being aware that paparazzi are blatantly following me or wondering whether someone is hiding behind a nearby lamppost – since camera-phones have been around anyone can just aim and shoot. It's something I've got used to over the years and there have been many times where a photographer's persistence has paid off and they've caught me looking like I've been dragged through a hedge backwards or while I'm having a mini-meltdown, which of course always makes it into the press. Just the thought of having a lens pointing at me while I was trying to breastfeed was enough to get me in a state. Once again I discussed my feelings with Lee and decided I would cross that bridge when I came to it – I would get the hang of feeding at home first and see how I felt then. I also called on my mates again who offered me the lowdown of mother-and-baby rooms in department stores that are perfect for discreet feeding. The funny thing is wherever I suggested I might be they already knew the best place nearby to breastfeed. I felt like I was being accepted into some kind of secret circle with all this specialist information!

I wanted to be as prepared as I could be so before I gave birth I had asked Becky to dedicate one of our antenatal classes solely to breastfeeding. Becky taught me that being relaxed was crucial and once I was comfortable it was all about getting in the right position to latch the baby on. The advice made perfect sense. We also covered the signs to look for to tell when your baby is hungry, how to prevent sore/cracked nipples and what to do if you get mastitis, which is a condition that occurs when the milk ducts get blocked and the breast tissue becomes inflamed and painful. Just the thought of it made me shiver. I also learned about some of the more weird and wonderful ways to cool sore nipples – who knew cabbage leaves could be quite so useful?!

Of course I shared everything with Lee and we discussed what was best for us as a couple. Being as brilliant as ever he was happy to support me with whatever I decided. All being well, when I had got the hang of breastfeeding I wanted to start expressing so he could help out with the night-time feeds to allow me to catch up on sleep. There's no denying that feeding your baby is really special, so Lee couldn't wait. The time he got home from working at the theatre would be perfect for him to do a late feed, plus expressing would be a good solution for me once I was back at work.

So with eight weeks to go before the birth, and with our ideal plan in place, I went out and bought everything I thought I would need: a few maternity bras, breast pads, nipple cream and so on. I did some research into the different pumps available and in the end went for the quietest one I could find because some of them sounded like they should be attached to a cow's udder! I cleared out yet another cupboard and filled it with all my purchases – my kitchen cupboards were slowly being taken over by baby stuff – but at least now I felt ready.

Not All Plain Sailing

To say my plans didn't quite go as expected would be a slight understatement. As soon as Betsy arrived, before I'd so much as thought about feeding her, I started experiencing searing pains in my nipples which felt like someone was sticking red-hot needles in them. So as you can probably imagine, when my midwife suggested I attempted to feed Betsy I was a little apprehensive.

Thankfully she had the patience of a saint and took time to show me the best way to position Betsy to get her to latch on. I can look back now and laugh at how comical it must have looked as I tried to aim this tiny face towards my enormous nipples. Mind you, they were so huge at this point it's surprising that Betsy could have missed. Despite all the preparation and practising I found it so difficult: as soon as I thought she had latched on and was feeding she'd pull away and start crying. I could feel the frustration building up inside both of us and I wanted to join Betsy in sobbing. The midwife helped to put it into perspective by saying it's like doing anything for the first time – you don't get behind the wheel of a car to find you have the skills of a Formula One driver or sit at a piano only to give Andrew Lloyd Webber a run for his money.

Of course she was right but I still felt frustrated. She assured me that Betsy wouldn't starve and I had plenty of time to get it right. She also suggested expressing a bit of milk into a cup by squeezing my breasts, which I did, and she helped me feed it to Betsy. I felt much better knowing that Betsy had drunk something and was able to close my eyes for a while to recharge my batteries. After a little snooze I tried again and this time was more successful. I discovered that the best position for me was to put my arm along Betsy's back and support her neck with my hand leaving her head free to bob about and find my nipple.

I was so happy that first day that I had managed to get her to latch on and was able to give her some of the amazing colostrum, the thick, nutrient-rich pre-milk, that I had read so much about. My friends had told me it would feel wonderful to have Betsy feeding from me and they were spot-on; the sense of achievement and satisfaction was unlike anything I'd ever felt. The closest feeling was the euphoria I experienced when I reached the top of Mount Kilimanjaro.

They say practice makes perfect and I did plenty of that over the next couple of days. Eventually, instead of me fumbling around for five or ten minutes trying to latch Betsy on for each feed, I got it down to under a minute before she was feeding away contentedly.

Throughout my pregnancy, I had watched in amazement as my boobs grew every day, wondering whether they would ever stop growing or even go pop! So they were pretty voluptuous by the time Betsy arrived and frankly I thought they couldn't get any bigger. Then, three days after Betsy was born, they literally doubled in size overnight and became very painful too. It looked like someone had grafted a couple of watermelons on to my chest! This was obviously what's referred to as the 'milk coming in' and even though it happens to everyone I certainly didn't expect it to feel like this. It was like going back to square one with feeding Betsy – I couldn't get her to latch on no matter how hard I tried. In the end I sat in a hot bath, placed a warm flannel over my boobs for a few minutes before squeezing some milk into the water to relieve the pressure. Just one squeeze and the milk kept on flowing – before I knew it my bath water was cloudy. I can't say I cared as the relief was amazing, like finally going to the loo when you've been desperate for hours. My little trick worked too: I was able to feed Betsy again afterwards (after more fumbling and crying on both our parts, of course).

Express Delivery

Over the next couple of weeks I began to enjoy feeding Betsy and I was surprised that it was the night feeds I enjoyed the most. Of course it's tiring waking up every few hours but I'd lie Betsy next to me in a fab feeding position I'd picked up in one of my books and just watch her feed in a cosy, semi-asleep state. However, there were a few nights in a row where I hardly got any sleep at all, so I decided to give expressing a go in the hope Lee could help out before I lost my marbles. It seemed that expressing was yet another art I was going to have to master because getting just a couple of ounces of milk took ages. I'm sure Betsy must have been getting her milk out much quicker otherwise she'd have been on my boob all day and night to get what she needed.

Eventually, after a few pumping sessions I managed to get enough for a full feed and Lee gave Betsy her first bottle – he loved it so much and Betsy didn't seem to mind drinking from a bottle in the slightest.

One funny side-effect of expressing was that I started to become really protective over my milk, probably because it was taking ages to get the smallest amount. On one occasion I had left some I had just expressed by the sink for no more than a couple of minutes while I dashed to the loo. Unfortunately it was long enough for Lee to spot the bottle, think it was left over from a feed and chuck it away. I was inconsolable for at least an hour. Poor Lee took the brunt of my despair until I'd calmed down, put it into perspective and apologised to him. He really did put up with a lot during this time.

For the first couple of weeks while we had visitors over I'd pop into my bedroom to feed Betsy so I didn't get stressed out trying to get it right in front of them and I could let it all hang out. This meant I was spending more time locked away than with our guests, so with the amount of milk increasing each time I expressed, I decided to try to express enough milk to bottle feed when we had people around. That way I didn't have to keep ducking into the bedroom and my mum – who was dying to feed Betsy – could help out.

Milk supply became a bit of a juggling act, as when Betsy wasn't feeding I would be pumping so we had enough stock in our fridge or freezer to keep us going. I felt as if I had something or someone attached to my nipples pretty much most of the time, but it was worth it. We got into a little routine – Lee would normally use my milk to feed Betsy during the night but if we ran low on expressed milk I would do those feeds myself until we caught up. One way or another I was beginning to feel that we'd cracked this whole breastfeeding lark.

Formula Won

Then when Betsy was around two and a half weeks old things changed. She wasn't sleeping well at all and was demanding to be fed constantly. We had exhausted our expressed milk supply and I was all over the place with sleep deprivation so we turned to formula for the odd feed as a temporary solution. It wasn't an easy decision as any breastfeeding mother will tell you – you want to provide the milk yourself and if you can't you feel a failure. As it turned out, Lee told me Betsy was knocking back almost double the amount we'd expected her to drink and was sleeping a lot longer as a result, which made me feel a lot better. I was actually beginning to think we had done the right thing in introducing some formula until Betsy started turning away from my nipple every time I tried to feed her. I tried everything I could think of to get her to latch on – I winded her, switched sides, changed positions and sat with her in a quiet environment. I didn't know what else to do and guessed that introducing formula had upset her in some way. As Betsy became more hungry she cried non-stop and we all started getting stressed out. In the end Lee sat me down and told me we needed to do something to stop both Betsy and I crying and he suggested I call my mum for advice.

My mum was great in calming me down before telling me that Betsy would be absolutely fine if I gave her formula and that I needed to stop being so hard on myself. After all, it wasn't the end of the world. She explained that she had found breastfeeding my sister relatively easy but struggled to keep up with the amount my brother was demanding (he's always been greedy) so switched to formula. By the time I came along she was so busy dashing around after three of us that I was formula-fed from the start.

Talking to my mum definitely helped but I still found making the decision to switch to formula really hard. I'd spent a couple of days feeling really down when my mate Jess called out of the blue to see how I was enjoying motherhood. I was glossing over the truth at first but as the call progressed I opened up and told her how I was really feeling. I hadn't realised that she had struggled with breastfeeding her little one too – I guess it's not something you bring up down the pub. We chatted for ages as she explained how she had been advised to introduce formula when her little boy Beau began losing weight. She went on to combination-feed him with breast and bottle until it got too much for her. She would breastfeed on one side then pump the other side in an attempt to boost her milk supply and would end up with very little milk for her effort. She told me she was consumed with feeding, pumping and timing feeds on her iPhone and was getting stressed out as a result. As in our case it was her husband who pointed this out and acted as a voice of reason, and once she switched to formula it felt like a huge weight had been lifted off her shoulders. She told me that looking back she feels that it was only at that point that she really began to enjoy being a mum.

Breastfeeding is one of those topics about which people are very passionate, and when it comes to parenting it's the one thing I have been judged on the most. I had my own demons to battle when we eventually decided to make the switch from breast to bottle when Betsy was three weeks old, but on top of that I received more than my fair share of criticism in the press. I was even misquoted in a magazine interview as saying I gave up breastfeeding because I didn't want to get my boobs out in Starbucks! Believe me, that was the last thing I was worrying about in the end.

It wasn't just the press who passed judgement either. Almost a month after I had stopped breastfeeding I received a letter from the NHS accompanied by a mug emblazoned with the slogan 'Keep Calm and Carry On Breastfeeding'. The letter suggested that Lee should be more supportive and if he were to make me more cups of tea using the mug they had kindly sent it would help me stay calm so I could continue to breastfeed. Really? If only someone had told me it was that easy before I spent over a hundred hours crying and tearing my hair out in desperation! What shocked and annoyed me the most was that having felt the need to defend myself following the negative press I had received, I had spoken publicly about the physical and emotional struggles I had encountered. The letter also made reference to my baby weight and the fact that breastfeeding would help me lose the weight quicker than if I formula-fed. I find it really sad that the NHS are sending out letters to new mums pretty much implying that they should lose weight. Do they really think that a new mum whose hormones are most likely running amok and is possibly feeling unhappy with her post-pregnancy figure needs to read such comments? I know for sure that I was feeling far from on top of the world and the arrival of the letter left me feeling even worse.

Despite my struggles with breastfeeding I am still a massive advocate and if anyone ever asks my opinion on the best way to feed their baby I'll always suggest giving breastfeeding a fair crack of the whip. However, my experiences have taught me that it shouldn't be taken for granted and formula-feeding should never be seen as 'failing'.

In any case, all of the reservations I had about formula-feeding Betsy soon disappeared as she began to grow into the amazing, active and intelligent young lady that she is today. Some of my fondest early memories are of watching Betsy knock back a big bottle of milk, getting 'milk drunk' in the process and spending the next few minutes with her eyes rolling with the cutest smile on her face. In the end she was growing and thriving – and that was the most important thing.

A word from my Twitter followers

Jenna, mum to a two-year-old

Breastfeeding is amazing if you are able to do it, but it isn't the end of the world if you can't. I tried my hardest but didn't succeed and was made to feel awful by some other mothers as a result.

Nina, mum to a five-year-old

I had seven weeks of HELL when breastfeeding my newborn. The pain was so unbearable I would cry at each feed. The health visitor told me I had poor attachment. It was only when I saw a doctor that I was diagnosed with thrush in my breasts.

Gina, mum to a sixteen-month-old son

My son was born three and a half weeks early and never learned to suckle properly as a result. Despite attending a breastfeeding support group I still struggled and finally gave up when he was ten weeks old. I felt so guilty and still do now.

Kara, mum to a two-year-old son

It's important not to get stressed out if your baby doesn't suckle straight away. Just ask the midwife to help you hand-express some breast milk so you can feed your baby with it and try again with the next feed. My baby wouldn't suckle at the breast for three days. As a midwife I found it frustrating being able to help other mums to breastfeed but not being able to do it myself. In the end I relaxed, persevered and breastfed for fourteen months.

Helen, mum to a six-month-old son

My mum encouraged me to breastfeed but when Maxx came along he was very sleepy following a seventeen-hour labour. He wasn't interested in feeding for the first sixteen hours so I didn't force him. Once the midwives found out how long he had gone without feeding they were worried and because he wouldn't latch on they cup-fed him some milk. My emotions were all over the place following the birth and the thought of not being able to breastfeed left me feeling devastated. I stayed in hospital for three nights while I got the hang of it and my sister-in-law, who is a midwife, visited to help me out. A lot of people who came and saw me struggling could not understand why I did not just give Maxx a bottle but my husband was incredibly encouraging and got me through the tough first days. I am sure that if it had not been for his support, Maxx would definitely be a bottle-fed baby now. I can honestly say that the whole breastfeeding process has been harder than the birth itself. But would I consider doing it again next time round? Absolutely.

Sarah, mum to a seven-month-old son

I was encouraged to breastfeed at my NCT classes and was determined to do it. A low-lying placenta scuppered my natural birth plans so skin-to-skin contact was my only hope of getting my hormones working and my milk flowing. Despite the help of midwives I couldn't get my baby to latch on or express any colostrum. Three days on and with bruised breasts where I had tried so hard to express, I was finally diagnosed with blocked milk ducts. I was both mentally and physically exhausted by this point. Still determined to breastfeed I visited a clinic and with their support I finally got the hang of it. My baby lost over 10 per cent of his birth weight, but by the time he was four weeks had gained it back and more. I did all the classes, read all the books but was never prepared for it not to work. It's the hardest thing I've ever done but also the most rewarding, and I will be ever thankful to the specialist breastfeeding counsellors who helped me.

Helen, mum to an eighteen-month-old girl

Ava breastfed immediately when she was born for fifty minutes and I thought, 'Wow! This is so easy!' Then she refused to feed at all for the next twenty-four hours. The midwives eventually discovered that it was because she had mucus on her tummy, which made her feel full. She had a good old vomit and was back feeding again with a vengeance. She fed pretty much all the time and her record was nine feeds over a single night. I loved breastfeeding and miss the intimacy and closeness now I've stopped. I don't miss getting the girls out in the night when it's freezing, though!

Claire, mum to two sons

I really struggled when it came to breastfeeding my first son and ended up sore and miserable after six weeks. Despite it feeling like my nipples were almost hanging off my health visitor told me I must have a low pain threshold! When my second son came along a friend suggested I used a cream called Lansinoh. It was amazing. I had no soreness and managed to breastfeed for six months, which I'm really proud of.

Anna, mum of three

When I fell pregnant with my first child I had heard stories about midwives not liking you to bottle-feed and doing everything in their power to persuade you to breastfeed. I couldn't think of anything worse. As much as I was excited and looking forward to having my baby, the thought of it hanging off my breast was a nightmare. I admire people who do it but I just couldn't get my head round it. My husband tried to make me feel guilty from time to time, saying the usual 'breastfeeding is best for the baby', but I was having none of it. When the midwife asked me how I was going to feed, I nipped it in the bud straight away and told her outright that I was bottle-feeding. She asked me if I was sure and whether I needed more time to think about it. I told her I definitely wanted to bottle-feed and to my surprise she never mentioned it again and didn't pester me at all.

Karen, mum to four-year-old and seven-year-old sons

I am very shy and knew that I would not be comfortable breastfeeding in front of my mam and dad, never mind complete strangers, so I made the decision immediately that I would bottle-feed my baby. I never told my midwife though, as I'd been told by a friend that they put huge pressure on you to breastfeed. I actually witnessed it for myself while at an antenatal class when the midwife turned on a poor woman, telling her she would damage her child. It confirmed my decision to keep quiet. Thankfully the hospital midwives were all lovely about my decision and didn't give me any hassle.

Chapter 5

Body Not So Beautiful?

Pregnancy and birth does funny things to your body and changes women in different ways. I have friends who are now much thinner than they were before they had kids, some of whom put it down to the lack of sleep and running around after their little ones, whereas others just can't explain it. I remember Victoria Beckham receiving stick when she was super-slim after one of her pregnancies, and there was a load of speculation about her unhealthy dieting and exercise regime to get back into shape. But she was adamant she hadn't been trying to lose so much weight and that it was the natural changes to her body post-birth that was making the weight loss happen so rapidly. Having been through some unexpected physical changes myself now, I totally believe her.

Pregnancy has changed my whole body. My hips are wider, my ribcage has expanded and my feet are a size bigger. It makes me sound like a clown, but it's the absolute truth and to be honest I wasn't expecting it at all. I don't remember reading anywhere that I might need to address my whole wardrobe after I'd given birth, yet many of my old outfits were still too much of a squeeze to get into (and even now, two years down the line, I still can't do the top button of my favourite jeans up). And don't even get me started on the fact that I may never be able to wear my fabulous shoe collection again. It brings a tear to my eye!

If I'm really honest I still don't feel like I've 'got my body back'. I feel like a woman who's had a baby – a bit 'mumsy' I suppose. But I don't know if that's just a mental thing or whether it is actually physiological and it worries me that I may never feel like I used to feel.

Weird and Wonderful Changes

Falling pregnant for the first time is bizarre. Most of the time, and certainly in my case, people are overjoyed for you and wish you nothing but love and happiness.

But oh my gosh! What I wasn't ready for were those people who feel it's their place to share their opinions with you whether you've asked for them or not. We've all experienced them – the person who tells you that you shouldn't be eating peanuts or tucking into that crayfish salad, a busybody who asks whether you should really be on the exercise bike in your condition or the taxi driver who swears blind it's a boy even though there is no way he could know. I couldn't believe how, almost overnight, I'd become public property, with even complete strangers chipping in with their opinions about my body.

Looking back now, I do understand it. When you've been through it yourself you want to share your experience with others. And, for the most part, I really liked getting advice and actually found it invaluable during what was a very alien and unnerving time. The insights from my mummy girlfriends and family were especially helpful, and I was always grateful to learn from them. I remember two subjects in particular kept coming up. Firstly, the physical discomfort you feel as your body adapts to carrying a baby and secondly, the anxiety you feel over losing your natural body shape. I know someone who was in so much pain towards the end of her pregnancy that just moving from her bed to the loo became a major mission, while another – who shall definitely remain nameless – said she had piles from week eight onwards and it took her two hours to poo!

Of course I experienced some strange changes to my body over the course of my pregnancy, but hearing these stories made me a thousand times more grateful that I had got off pretty lightly. Whereas many of my mummy mates suffered with heartburn and morning sickness (it still baffles me why it's called morning sickness by the way, when those unlucky enough to suffer from it often feel nauseous morning, noon and night), the majority of the time I felt absolutely fine as long as I ate sensibly and didn't go too long without food.

Before you all start muttering 'you lucky cow', I didn't get away with it completely scot-free. Towards the end of my pregnancy, and in particular the last week, so many of my body parts had swollen I could have easily acted as a body double for Gwyneth Paltrow in *Shallow Hal*. My feet suffered the most, swelling up so much that Lee and I affectionately renamed them my luncheon feet. Similarly my calves and ankles took on a life of their own, conspiring to create one entity: my cankles! For someone used to dancing and prancing round onstage I can tell you that by my final month of pregnancy I was desperate to feel light on my feet again and replace the thud in my step with a spring. My face had also swollen, giving me a double chin and making me look like I'd seriously piled on the pounds. Thankfully within a couple of hours of Betsy arriving my legs and face had started to change back. Although not everything was quite so quick to spring back to normal...

Tummy Trouble

OK, now be honest with me, how many of you first-time mums out there thought that after nine months of continual growing you'd give birth and your belly would revert back to its old shape in no time at all? I know I made that mistake! Call me naïve but I thought that once Betsy had made her grand entrance into the world there would be nothing in my stomach to make it stick out any more. How wrong was I? As soon as I was up on my feet in the hospital I looked down to find I still looked six months pregnant! For a split second I actually wondered whether there was another baby in there.

I joked with Lee that my puffy uterus made me look like a Stormtrooper but secretly I was worried that my tummy might never look the same again. I remember asking the midwives about it and they reassured me that it takes around four weeks for your uterus to contract back to its normal size. I spent a good four or five days wandering around slightly disappointed that I was still the shape of a beach ball before things began moving in the right direction and my bump slowly started to disappear.

Elasticated Waistbands

Like most girls I love a bit of shopping, so in the really early stages of pregnancy when my normal clothes were getting a bit tighter I looked forward to the shopping trips dedicated to updating my wardrobe with all things elasticated. I couldn't wait to put on my first pair of trousers with an elasticated waist – it felt like my pregnancy was receiving an official seal of approval. It wasn't long until the novelty had worn off though, and I started to find it really difficult to get clothes that were fashionable and affordable. Luckily for me I was asked to work with the guys at the online department store, Very, to help design a range of maternity clothes to try to rectify this. Once their soft jersey samples started coming through it was as if I had my own custom-made wardrobe, just for me, and these saw me through the rest of my pregnancy.

Pregnancy does funny things to some people, though, and can make even the most stylish of people lose their mojo. I'll never forget Katie Price's audition for Eurovision back in 2005, for a number of reasons – but mainly because she wore a skin-tight pink Lycra catsuit while heavily pregnant. Not my cup of tea. On the other hand I felt inspired by plenty of celebs who have managed to look stylish throughout their pregnancy – Mylene Klass always looks fantastic, preggers or not, and Rachel Stevens also looked great while sporting her bump.

That said, as my due date neared I did start to get more and more excited about dressing in normal clothes again. By the time I was eight months pregnant I remember feeling that if I never saw an elasticated waistband again, it would be too soon. If it wasn't for the guilt I'd have felt for being wasteful, I swear I would have lit a bonfire in my back garden and got rid of all my maternity clothes in one fell swoop. I felt like it would have given me the same sort of glimpse of freedom the women's rights campaigners felt when they burnt their bras in the sixties. Still, with my big belly and wider hips there was no way I was fitting into any of my normal clothes for a while so my maternity wardrobe had a brief reprieve at least.

When I did eventually have a big clear out and passed on my maternity clothes to a pregnant friend who couldn't wait to slip into my elasticated jeans (she soon changed her tune), a few items survived. I still wear my maternity tracky bottoms and baggy T-shirts to bed now – much to Lee's dismay.

Taking Things Slowly (Well, Trying to)

For any woman who has just given birth, no matter how fit or healthy you are, it's important to take things slowly. You have to let your body recover a bit, and let's face it, ladies, you'd be hard-pushed to find a better reason to justify switching down a gear or two for a few weeks than having a newborn to coo over.

As I had Betsy by Caesarean I was under strict instructions to take it easy for at least twelve weeks and when I left hospital I had the best intentions of taking plenty of rest. The plan was to spend my days lounging on the sofa, Betsy in my arms, with a cup of tea to hand.

Who was I kidding? I find sitting still for twelve minutes impossible, let alone twelve weeks! I promise you I did try to take it easy but sitting watching the dust settle started to drive me crackers and anyone who knows me well will tell you I'm crazy about cleaning. Give me a pair of Marigolds and a bottle of Flash and I'm in heaven. So I was soon darting around the house in a cleaning frenzy catching up on what I'd been missing out on for the last few weeks.

If I had felt any pain I would have rested but moving around helped me feel better. I was careful not to over-exert myself and I certainly wasn't going to do any strenuous exercise in an attempt to get back into shape quickly. I just wanted nature to take its course. I didn't put any pressure on myself to lose my baby weight and in fact I still haven't weighed myself post-birth to this day. I admit this wasn't just down to willpower: bizarrely I came home from the hospital after giving birth to Betsy to find that our bathroom scales had mysteriously broken. I took it as a sign that I wasn't to stress over how much I weighed.

Healthy Is Key

To be really honest, if I had fallen pregnant when I was younger I'd have been much harder on myself. I'd have wanted to lose any baby weight I'd gained as quickly as possible and I'd have skipped meals or reduced my portion sizes a little too much. As I've got older I've realised it's much more important to focus on being healthy rather than being thin. I feel sorry for young celebrities who are in the public eye at the moment because there is so much emphasis placed on size. Back when I was presenting *The Big Breakfast* and was doing plenty of press interviews there weren't magazines like *Heat*, *Closer* and *Reveal* so there wasn't this obsession with bodies. No one ever asked me about my weight or what I ate, which I'm quite glad about as I was regularly indulging in the full works: eggs, bacon, sausage, fried bread ... a proper big breakfast!

These days there are features in magazines dedicated to highlighting celebrities' weight gain and recounting the struggles they are experiencing to get back in shape after they've had a baby. I can see why celebs feel the pressure to bounce back to their pre-pregnancy weight as quickly as possible because the last thing anyone wants is to be criticised for being overweight, especially when they are feeling vulnerable post-birth. On the other hand though, if someone in the public eye loses weight too quickly they also get stick for being a bad role model. You're damned if you do and damned if you don't, so you may as well just be healthy and happy, that's what I say.

I remember watching an interview with Joan Collins where she was asked how she has managed to keep in such great shape and look so youthful over the years. She revealed her secret was to never get too thin because it doesn't look womanly and it ages you. I think she looks amazing for her age so I'm happy to do it the Joan way.

I must admit to being extremely fortunate as I've inherited my dad's slim frame. Over the years my weight has only really fluctuated a few pounds so I was pretty sure that my body would bounce back fairly quickly with the right exercise and a healthy diet. When I wasn't busying myself with the cleaning I took plenty of gentle walks to keep moving. Sometimes I'd take Betsy with me and occasionally my mum would come over so I could escape on my own. My first experience of mother's guilt was when I popped out and left Betsy, who was almost two weeks old, at home with my mum. It felt like I was bunking off school and I spent the whole time worrying only to return to find she had been fast asleep for the entire duration. I didn't go quite as mad as Victoria Beckham who reportedly walked seven miles a day (surely that would take the whole day!) after the birth of her daughter Harper Seven; mine was just a gentle stroll to the high street or to the park which was enough to stretch my legs and clear my head. Thankfully the shortness of breath I had suffered towards the end of my pregnancy had disappeared now that my lungs were no longer being squashed, which meant I could at least take a stroll without sounding like I had a part-time job as a dirty phone-line operator.

Healthy Diet

As I put my mind to it over a lovely – if slightly larger than it used to be – lunch, I realised the cravings for carbs and fatty food that I had experienced while pregnant had actually developed into an ongoing eating habit. I'd got rather too used to tucking into big bowls of pasta, cheese and anything I fancied throughout my pregnancy, whereas now all of a sudden I needed to be more calorie-conscious again (especially later after I stopped breastfeeding and no longer needed those extra 500 calories a day). It took serious willpower to stick to a healthy diet as every single visitor who came to see Betsy came bearing gifts of the edible variety. My kitchen work surfaces were lost under a sea of cakes, biscuits and chocolates, which may sound like heaven but when you're trying to be good it's a nightmare.

One of my girlfriends, Jessica, was so careful about what she ate while she was pregnant that two days after giving birth she was back to her exact pre-preggers weight.

It was only when the tiredness kicked in and she started getting together with the other mums from her NCT group for coffee and cakes that her weight started creeping up once more. She wasn't amused when her clothes started getting tight on her again!

A common if unexpected side effect of having a baby is that the new dad piles on the pounds too. This happened to us: while I exercised my willpower, Lee was merrily tucking into the goody mountain each night when he came home from the theatre. In no time at all he was having difficulty fitting into some of his more slim-fitting clothes and he wasn't happy. To my great amusement, he was the one now having to go on a diet. I guess constant gifts of chocolates and cake coupled with no desire to leave your newborn to visit the gym is a recipe for weight gain. On the plus side, if you're dieting together at least there'll be no cheeky takeaways or stashes of cheese in the fridge. There's nothing worse than nibbling on a carrot while your other half is devouring a huge fry-up.

Wedding Belle

I've always found that having a goal to work towards helps me stick to a healthy diet and fitness regime, and goals don't get much better than having a fancy showbiz wedding to attend just two weeks after having a baby. This really was just what I needed to motivate me, especially as it was my good friend David Walliams who was tying the knot. I knew for certain that turning up on his big day would be more like a red-carpet event than a low-key wedding so I wanted to look the best I could.

With my tummy feeling and looking like jelly it was important for me to choose my outfit wisely. I started with the appropriate undies – a big support bra and a pair of full-length Spanx, which could easily be mistaken for cycling shorts rather than underwear. They may not look so glamorous in the raw but they do an amazing job, coming right up to the bust line and squeezing everything inwards and upwards.

David's wedding was the first proper day out Lee and I had had since Betsy arrived and on the run-up to it we'd been getting really excited about getting dressed up and spending a few hours together as a couple. Just the day before, Lee had seen my dress hanging up in the bedroom and had commented that I was going to look stunning in it. So you can presumably picture his face when he walked into our bedroom as I was right in the middle of hauling, squeezing and wriggling myself into what resembled a full-length Tubigrip. Hands down the most unattractive underwear he'd ever seen me in by a mile. As he retreated sharpish to the kitchen I'm sure he was thinking he was now sentenced to a life of viewing his wife in boulder-holder bras and granny knickers.

Once my dress was on – a little number cut on the bias (another little figure-flattering trick) – my undies were forgotten and I was really happy with the way I looked. My mum was looking after Betsy for the three hours or so we'd be out, so I gave her a quick run-down of everything she would need – I'd left a bottle of expressed milk in the fridge and stocked up the drawers of Betsy's change table with nappies and wipes. My mum smiled as I went over everything in minute detail. No doubt the phrase 'teaching granny to suck eggs' sprang to her mind, but she knew it would make me feel better to get it all off my chest.

As we pulled up outside the super-posh Claridge's Hotel where David was getting hitched, my heart was pounding so hard. I was unusually nervous as it was the first time I'd been seen out since having Betsy. The newspapers can be really harsh and are ready to pounce if you don't look good and I knew there would be photographers waiting to get a shot of me post-birth. As I opened the car door I took a deep breath in and held it as I stood with Lee (who looked dashingly handsome, I must add) while the photographers flashed away. Once inside the entrance I let out the loudest gasp as I struggled for air – the things us ladies do. The day was wonderful and I was over the moon to be on the receiving end of many lovely compliments on how good I looked so soon after becoming a mum.

Use Achievements to Spur You on

The compliments made me feel great and they made me even more determined to lay off the muffins and brownies – a bit like when you start a diet and people begin to compliment you on your weight loss. It makes you feel inspired and motivated to keep up the good work. And it was just as well I had the 'eye of the tiger' (cue theme tune) because there was just one week before I had to model the maternity range I had designed for Very – and as they say, the camera never lies!

Betsy was just three weeks old when I did my first day's work, a photo shoot for the Very website. A couple of days before the shoot I felt slightly nervous at the thought of leaving the comfort of the baby bubble I had been living in since Betsy arrived. I certainly didn't feel ready to leave her at home all day with Lee, not because I doubted his ability to look after her – I knew she would have been cuddled from the moment I left until I returned – but because I wasn't sure *I* could last for more than five minutes without her. After weighing up my options I decided I would feel happier taking Betsy with me, so I invited my best mate Tamara to come along to help out.

The morning of the photo shoot was chaotic. Normally when I have a shoot I'll pack a bag the night before containing shoes and underwear to go with various outfits, but on this occasion I'd left it until the last minute. In any case, now it was all about Betsy. As I remembered one thing after another I needed to take for her the pile on my bed got bigger and bigger. Once I'd finished getting her things together you would have been excused for thinking we were off on a two-week holiday we had so much baggage.

The one thing I did remember to pack for myself was my trusty pair of Spanx, to hold in my jelly belly. The dresses I'd designed could be worn both during pregnancy and after having a baby so we had two lovely pregnant models to show what the dresses looked like on a pregnant figure while I struck the post-birth pose. The Spanx came in useful to smooth out any remaining lumps and bumps in my figure.

I wasn't too worried about stripping off even though my body was unrecognisable compared to what it looked like ten months ago. I had a valid excuse, having given birth just three weeks ago. Besides, my make-up artist Emma would be the only person to see me in my undies and she has two children so totally understands that things go a bit awry for a while. I was more worried about my C-section scar, which had become infected, making it itchy and sore, so I had to be careful not to scratch or knock it and keep it covered up.

I had really missed feeling pampered so relished every minute of having my hair and make-up done. Betsy loved meeting everyone working on the shoot, most of whom I had known for ages and who had witnessed my ever-increasing bump during my pregnancy. In fact it's fair to say Betsy was the star of the day, getting in on some of the pictures and being cuddled to within an inch of her life.

It was great to see everyone again and I was pleased I had managed to do the shoot while Betsy was with me without any real dramas. The only time I did question whether I had done the right thing was when she started crying and wouldn't stop. It took a while to settle her and I felt a bit self-conscious but she was fine in the end. Despite it being work it felt more like pleasure and helped me feel like normal again after having spent the last three weeks wondering how this little girl was going to change my life.

My high of getting back out into the real world was short-lived, however, as I returned home that evening to read what people had written about me on Twitter. I had posted a message earlier in the day saying: 'Back to work – have a shoot for my Very maternity range.' There were lots of lovely tweets from people wishing me luck but there were also some really nasty ones. People had written things about me being a bad mum for working so soon after having a baby. The one that sticks in my mind the most said: 'Leaving your baby at home so soon! Shame on you.' I then tweeted to say that Betsy had come with me and they started again: 'That's no place for a baby!' To say I came crashing back down to earth with a thud would be the understatement of the century.

I know it's ridiculous – having worked in the public eye for as long as I have, you'd think I'd have developed thicker skin and learned to ignore people who are nasty or negative, especially when they don't know me personally. But the criticism really got to me – there's something about being criticised as a mum that hits you much harder – and I spent the whole evening and following day really upset because people I've never met decided they had the right to judge me.

Mummy Meltdown

It was just after the Very shoot on my birthday on 27 May that I experienced my first 'mummy meltdown'. We'd had so much going on up until that point, what with the constant stream of visitors, David's wedding plus the building work outside the flat to contend with, that I guess all the stress and tension had built up without me realising. I had planned a small girly get-together in the evening at a restaurant on the high street as I thought it would be good for me to get out, and I had asked my mum to babysit. But my day was a nightmare and Betsy cried continually. In addition, I knew that I needed to learn three songs in preparation for my audition for the role of Princess Fiona in the new West End musical *Shrek*. The American producers were flying into London for the auditions and had specifically requested to see me.

It would have been a fantastic role to get but I didn't have any time to listen to the songs, let alone learn the words off by heart. When my then agent called I explained that I was having difficulty finding time, plus I didn't have anyone to look after Betsy when I was supposed to be at the audition. She was really keen for me not to miss out on such a fantastic opportunity, and so that I could find some time to learn the songs and do the audition even suggested that if I couldn't find a babysitter I could drop Betsy off at the office so everyone there could look after her. I'm sure she meant well, but there was just no way I could have left my newborn baby with strangers while I went off and auditioned, something I'm sure a lot of new mums will understand. I had no option but to pull out of the audition as the last thing I wanted was to come across as underprepared and unprofessional. I knew it was the right thing to do but I couldn't help but feel as though I had let everyone down, myself included.

At two o'clock on my birthday I found myself completely exhausted. I sat on my unmade bed with Betsy still crying in my arms, and out of nowhere I felt a wave of emotion wash over me and I burst into tears. Once the floodgates were open that was it and I cried continually for three hours. My phone rang and beeped with 'happy birthday' messages but I didn't move, I just sat there sobbing.

When I finally stopped, my eyes were so red and swollen I could hardly recognise myself when I looked in the mirror. I put Betsy in her Moses basket as she had fallen asleep and ran myself a bath. I thought this would cheer me up, but the floodgates opened again (I'm sure my bathwater level rose a few inches) and they continued until my friend Julie arrived on my doorstep at six o'clock. Bless her, there she was all cheery and glammed up to celebrate with me and I opened the door to greet her looking like the world was about to end.

She made me a cup of tea – which, let's face it, makes everything all right – and listened as I poured out how I was feeling. A sympathetic ear seemed to do the trick and Julie somehow persuaded me to get ready and meet up with my girlfriends as planned. I'm so lucky to have a really close group of friends who I can be myself with. As we laughed about my puffy eyes over a glass of wine, the dramas of the day faded away. My mum sent me regular Betsy updates via text, saying things like, 'She's out like a light' and 'Still in the land of nod', which helped to put my mind at rest.

The following morning though, as I ran through what had happened the previous day, I decided it was too much for me to be a good mum to Betsy and to deal with the stresses of having a career too. I had no choice but to stop working. Of course I wasn't thinking rationally at the time and hadn't really thought about how the mortgage would get paid – after all, it's not like I work for a company and would receive maternity pay. I hadn't even considered what Lee would have to say on the matter; my head was just all over the place.

Luckily my publicist Simon called me for a chat before I had the chance to call my agent to tell her I didn't want to work any more. He helped me put everything into perspective and told me I needed to take time out so that my hormones could return to normal. The auditions and work could wait. He was right. I realised what I really needed to do was ease some of the pressure off, taking some time out to enjoy motherhood before returning fully to work only when the time felt right – and that's exactly what I did.

It's natural for new mums to feel quite vulnerable at first as they get to grips with their new role and with the baby blues taking hold of me at this time I felt more fragile than most. The unfamiliarity of becoming a mum, crazy hormones, change in lifestyle and lack of sleep had all hit me hard and left me not only doubting myself, but also sapped of any mental energy.

When my hormones eventually settled down after around three months and I began to feel like myself again I started to take the odd job when I felt up to it, but most of the time I spent with Betsy. It proved to be the right move because it allowed me to become more comfortable with being a mum and to find the right balance. I love my work – it can be hard at times but it's exciting and makes me happy and I need that in my life. It's not only good for my own sanity but it makes me feel like a better mum to Betsy too, because now she's bigger being away from her – even just for a few hours – makes me treasure every minute I'm with her even more.

A word from my Twitter followers

Kelly, mum to a one-year-old son

When I was pregnant with my first baby I wore Shape Ups trainers and I swear that this was the reason I put on hardly any weight. I walked to and from the station right up until my thirty-seventh week. The only maternity clothes I bought were bump bands and I stayed in my size-eight jeans all the way through the pregnancy and fitted right back into them the day I gave birth! I'd certainly recommend the trainers to anyone because I ate like a horse. I am pregnant again now and I hardly look pregnant.

Leila, mum to a three-year-old son

It's taken three years to reclaim back most of my body and the rest has been hopefully hidden well enough so that no one has noticed. When I think back I was so paranoid about the stretch marks but now realise they were the least of my problems. I spent nine months whilst pregnant listening to my friends who told me I needed to eat for two, rest for two and take it easy for two. So I would happily get in from work, scoff a plate full of comfort food and a bit of chocolate to get baby kicking, and then put my feet up in front of the TV. I instantly regretted this once I had my son Oliver. My bladder lost all control, I had haemorrhoids the size of marbles and constipation so bad I didn't 'go' for nearly four weeks. My problems worsened and led to infections. After six weeks I was diagnosed with a small bowel prolapse and I've been told that as I want more children it isn't worth rectifying the problem. It was recommended I started doing some gentle exercise to strengthen my pelvic floor. I have never stopped going to the gym since and I'm amazed at how much I have recovered. Any future pregnancy will consist of healthy eating, sitting upright to keep the best posture and lots of exercise. I will also be making sure I am well prepared for a slow recovery afterwards. Still, I wouldn't change anything for the world as I now have my little boy who I adore.

Joanne, mum of two

Sixteen years later and I have never got my body back. I'm only thirty-three, it's a killer – trust me!

Emma, mum to a three-year-old son

I am just over five months' pregnant again now and would love to 'bloom' and enjoy pregnancy but my body is having none of it. I was constipated for six weeks at the start, and I'm now suffering with heartburn and indigestion. During my last pregnancy I got abscesses in the base of my spine at six months – I'm hoping those don't return! Despite all this though, I am so happy to be pregnant again, and seeing my belly wiggle around with the movements of my baby inside is the loveliest thing ever. A washboard tummy was replaced with a proper muffin-top, wobbler of a stomach first time round – but I don't mind, it's all worth it!

Natasha, mum to a four-year-old son

While I was pregnant I loved every bit of it and was only uncomfortable during the last couple of weeks before giving birth. After having my baby I hated my body, I wouldn't let my partner see me naked and wouldn't get intimate. It was so bad that my partner and I split up and I still hate my body four years later. Nothing I do will get rid of my baby belly. I am a working single mum and don't have the money or time to go to the gym or employ a personal trainer. I'm worried I will hate my body forever.

Davynia, mum to a twenty-month-old

No one really warns you about how your bladder is so weak afterwards. It's been twenty months now and I'm back at the gym, but I feel I can never give 100 per cent while I'm working out as I'm worried about what might happen down there.

Danielle, mum to a six-year-old daughter and three-year-old son

After years of eating healthy and being a gym bunny I decided that pregnancy was my excuse to 'relax' my healthy lifestyle. BIG mistake! I ended up putting on four stone, which took my two years to lose, and I was left with diastasis of the abdominal muscles! I have recently given birth to my second child and had a much more healthy pregnancy. I continued going to the gym three times a week until a week before my due date and was back at the gym three and a half weeks after she was born. I have now lost all my baby weight and weigh the same as I did before I had my first child. I still have split abdominals though and extremely saggy skin on my stomach from my first pregnancy. My doctor has told me the only likely solution is surgery, which is sad as I'm only twenty-six! I'm trying my best to do Pilates-type exercises but nothing seems to be improving my tummy.

Chapter 6

Bye Bye Baby

When Betsy was only four and a half months old I was faced with a real dilemma. Before she was even a twinkle in her daddy's eye I'd made arrangements with my pal Fearne Cotton to do a charity trek across the Andes to Machu Picchu with a group of breast cancer survivors. Even way back then, it was a huge goal for me to get fit for but now just the thought of it was enough to bring me out in a cold sweat. I wasn't going to let the physical challenge deter me though, as Breast Cancer Care is such an important cause to me, having lost my beloved nan to the disease a few years ago.

I knew I needed to be on top form if I was going to enjoy the trek without struggling. Not only was I to be joined by a team of female celebrities but also a group of women who had undergone intensive and debilitating cancer treatment – and they had managed to get themselves fit enough to make the trek. The last thing I wanted was to hold everyone up by being too slow, or even worse, see a shot of my hefty rear in tight Lycra being shown on national TV. Like most women I have plenty of insecurities about how I look and how people perceive me, and when I'm going to be surrounded by an amazing array of strong and beautiful cancer survivors and a bunch of gorgeous celebrity females including Fearne Cotton, Alexandra Burke and Amanda Byram I felt like I really needed to up my game.

I had four months to prepare for what would be, alongside climbing Mount Kilimanjaro, one of the biggest challenges of my life. Once more I called on the expert help of my friend and personal trainer Nicki Waterman who has helped me to get fit for many roles and events over the years. She designed a training schedule that increased my exercise slowly but ensured I would be fit enough for the trek in September. We walked on trails through woodlands and countryside in order to get used to trekking over stones and uneven ground, wearing the hiking boots I'd be using for the trip and carrying a rucksack. I also swam and ran twice a week and included some strength training to beef up my arms, shoulders, back and abdominals.

Getting It in Perspective

The training paid off and I not only survived the trek but had a life-changing experience by spending time with such inspirational women. The biggest lesson I learned was the importance of not blowing everything out of proportion. A couple of days into the trek I woke up absolutely dreading what lay ahead. All of the other girls had been getting excited about stopping off at some hot springs for a dip on our way to the next camp and had mentioned that they had their bikinis at the ready. The thought of having to put my swimming costume on in front of the girls terrified me. Everyone knows that I can talk for England but with this on my mind I was unusually quiet as the other girls joked and chatted away. I had packed my one-piece swimming costume just in case I needed it but was still far from ready to put it on.

When we arrived at the spot I sat chatting to Lou, one of the ladies who had survived cancer, and confided in her that I was dreading stripping off because I was still not happy with my post-pregnancy figure. She sat and listened as my insecurities flooded out before confiding in me that she had been feeling nervous too as she had undergone a mastectomy. She went on to tell me how she tried not to let minor things like how she looked or how people perceived her worry her any more, as she's just grateful to be alive.

Wow, talk about an eye-opening conversation. She was absolutely right, of course. I had so many things to be grateful for: a gorgeous daughter, good health and I was in an amazing place with fabulous company. The last thing I should be doing is stressing over how I was going to look in a swimming cozzie. After our chat I went back to my tent and burst into tears in front of Fearne as I told her what had just happened. I felt like such an idiot and angry at myself for worrying about such a trivial thing.

Once I'd composed myself I put on my costume and joined the rest of the ladies in the springs. Some of us were wearing costumes and others were covering up with T-shirts. We all chatted and laughed and it was actually one of the highlights of my trip and a memory I'll cherish. I learned that day that the majority of things we worry about just don't really matter and there's always someone whose problems will make your worries seem trivial.

Separation Anxiety (Mine)

The other big issue of the trip I had to deal with, of course, was leaving Betsy for seven days. I'd organised the trek before I was even pregnant but the timing of it meant I had to fly to South America when she was still very young. I don't deny that it was early to leave her and believe me it was something I thought long and hard about, but after weighing everything up I decided it was important for me to keep my commitment and raise much-needed awareness and money for Breast Cancer Care. As the day of my departure drew nearer, there were times I almost pulled out, but breast cancer has had such a devastating effect on my family I was determined to honour my commitment.

In an attempt to put my mind at rest I asked a few of my mummy friends for advice. The majority told me that when a baby is just a few months old and is separated from its mum, it's the mother who suffers the most. In fact the consensus seemed to be that the baby pretty much carries on as normal as long as it's left with close family members. Lee had taken the week off and my mum was staying at ours too so I knew Betsy would be in safe and loving hands. Even so, the night before I left I lay in bed with Lee and bawled my eyes out, questioning what I was even thinking flying five and a half thousand miles away from Betsy. It didn't get any easier on my way to the airport. After a sleepless night I was all over the place – my poor driver must have thought the world was going to end the way I was carrying on in the back of his cab.

Unfortunately I didn't get to speak to Lee and Betsy the entire week as I was in the middle of nowhere without a telephone signal. I did receive a video message from them via the crew that were filming us for a TV documentary. I was so happy to see them that I blubbered for a good hour or so afterwards.

I had plenty of fantastic people around me to lift my spirits if I was missing Lee and Betsy – Fearne and Amanda would constantly crack jokes. I also spent a lot of time chatting to Lou, the lady who I had spoken to before the hot springs, who had left her five-year-old son at home and was missing him like crazy too. Lou was suffering from secondary breast cancer (unfortunately, she found a lump when eight months' pregnant, and despite going through all the treatments, the cancer had spread to another area of her body), so she signed up for the trek because she wanted to do something to raise awareness of the awful disease. Listening to her story of her battle with breast cancer and how she has had to come to terms with the possibility that she may not see her little boy grow up put everything in perspective as far as me leaving Betsy for a week was concerned. She's such a brave and inspirational woman. We have remained friends after our trip and have agreed that when our little ones are old enough to understand we'd show them the pictures and videos from our time in Peru and make them proud of us.

Although the trek was hard work and it seemed a long week away, when I got home my lovely Betsy was all smiles and hugs and within minutes it felt like I hadn't been anywhere. Once again I was greeted by negative comments on Twitter, this time saying I was a bad mum for swanning off to Peru and leaving Betsy when she was so young. It obviously wasn't nice to read but I knew I'd made the right decision in going. With impeccable timing Lou tweeted me to say she was really upset to read the negative comments and judgements I had received and wanted to thank me for doing the trek for Breast Cancer Care. Every single one of the negative comments I'd received paled into insignificance in light of the positive affirmation of someone with the strength and grace of Lou.

Nanny SOS

When I returned home from the trek I felt stronger than ever, not surprisingly given that I'd just spent a week hiking for six to nine hours a day across the Andes. Just as well really, as the day after I got home I had a brand-new challenge to face – I was due to start rehearsals for the West End musical *Legally Blonde*. Talk about surreal: just thirty-six hours previously I was standing among the ruins of Machu Picchu, and now there I was first thing on a Monday morning in the heart of London learning a big Irish dance number.

With this exciting new development, though, came a new headache: sorting out childcare. Lee and I are extremely lucky as our careers often give us plenty of time to spend with Betsy, especially when we have roles in the West End, because we are generally around in the daytime. Our hours are often unpredictable though, which means childcare needs to be flexible too. When we're doing theatre it's the afternoons and evenings where we need help with looking after Betsy, which is obviously way outside of crèche or nursery opening hours – so that wasn't an option. I would have loved to have had a family member, especially my mum, to look after Betsy for us as I remember she really helped my sister out with her little ones. But that was a few years ago when my mum was younger; she's now in her late sixties and would find looking after Betsy too much on a regular basis. She still comes over to stay once a week and spends the whole day with us but even then I can see she's exhausted by the time she comes to leave.

So after much discussion Lee and I decided that it was time for us to get a nanny. It was a huge decision as it meant trusting our precious daughter, and our home, to someone who would for all intents and purposes be a complete stranger at first.

I did an insane amount of research, speaking to friends and family and spending hours discussing it with Lee. In the end I went with a friend's suggestion: my mate Karen found her nanny via a local agency and highly recommended it to me. It gave me peace of mind that Karen had already dealt with them as it was slightly nerve-racking to think that I was trusting this company to vet suitable candidates. But I felt it was the right thing to do: I'd always advise using an agency because then you know that the nannies' references are fully checked and that they've had the correct medical training. I duly contacted the agency and they lined up some potential candidates for us to interview.

Lee and I put together a list of what we were looking for – someone who'd be delicate with Betsy, who wouldn't try to take over and who was fun to be around. I arranged to meet three nannies in the hope that one of them would fit the bill. The first nanny was lovely but she wasn't as gentle as I would have liked when she picked up Betsy to say hello. The next nanny was too young – I felt I wanted someone with a bit more experience, not just so she could keep Betsy safe but also in the hope she would have lots of tried-and-tested fun activities up her sleeve.

The last candidate was forty-seven-year-old Feni. The first thing that struck me was how happy she was; she spoke softly to Betsy and she clearly loved kids as she also worked part-time in a local nursery. Even better she came with great references and would often still babysit for the families she had worked for in the past. I was really impressed so invited her to spend the day with the family at our flat.

Upon meeting her Lee also thought she was lovely and as the day progressed we drank tea while filling her in on Betsy's routine and the things she liked to do. By the end of the day we decided Feni was our girl and took the plunge by signing her up. In the end you need to trust your instincts when you meet potential candidates and both Lee and I had a good feeling about Feni.

My favourite time of the day with Betsy is bath and bedtime – it's such a special bonding time and a chance for one last play before bed. Putting my little angel down at night means the world to me, but with me needing to be at the theatre for five o'clock and Betsy having a set bedtime routine we were keen to stick to, Feni would have to take over. I was gutted but it was a sacrifice I would have to make, at least until my theatre run came to an end. Every working mum has to forfeit one thing or another: mums who work nine to five miss lunchtimes and trips to the park. It's just one of those things.

The first evening we left Betsy with Feni, Lee and I both had to work. I was much more confident about it than Lee was, perhaps because I'd spent more time with Feni and spoken to her more often. Lee was quite panicky so I had to be strict with him and tell him that under no circumstances was he to call home during the evening to check up, as if there was a problem Feni would call us. I must admit, however, I felt a bit anxious myself on my way home from the theatre and couldn't wait to get into the flat once my cab pulled up outside.

I opened the door to the welcome sight of a big smile from Feni, which instantly put me at ease. She told me Betsy had been as good as gold during her bath time, went down without any problems and had been sleeping without so much as a peep for the last four hours. Thankfully, after leaving Betsy for the first time it got much easier and Feni soon became part of our family, looking after Betsy until she started nursery.

When All's Not Well

There are of course times when it's really hard to leave Betsy, especially when she's feeling under the weather and needs her mummy more than ever. There was one occasion when Betsy was six months old and she wasn't feeling well and had been clingy all day. I had to practically drag myself out the door to go to work, leaving my mum to look after her. An hour or so after I'd left, Betsy developed a rash and her temperature rose to over thirty-nine degrees. Wanting to be on the safe side my mum decided to take her to hospital to get her checked out. My mum has never visited an A&E department in her life and figured it to be much like a doctor's surgery – wait for twenty minutes before you see a doctor and then head home with a prescription. She certainly thought they would be back home before I returned from the theatre. How wrong could she have been – she was there for hours.

When I got home to an empty flat I was beside myself with worry and desperate to find out what had happened. I called my mum first but there was no answer, then I tried Lee's phone, which went straight to voicemail. Eventually I got hold of my dad who filled me in. At first I was really annoyed that my mum hadn't called or at least sent a text message to let me know what was happening but once I was thinking rationally again I realised she had just done what she thought was best for Betsy. Thankfully there was nothing seriously wrong and Betsy was right as rain the next day. It was me who was suffering by the end of the drama – I had a splitting headache and lay awake for most of the night wishing I had followed my instincts by staying at home with Betsy instead of going to work. And you've guessed it – I felt guilty!

After I finished my stint in *Legally Blonde* I had hoped to take my foot off the pedal a little so I could spend more time at home with Betsy but as is always the case when you don't really want work that's precisely when it comes along, often in the form of an offer that's too good to refuse. True to form, I was offered a role in a film, a comedy called *Run for Your Wife*, by the fantastic director Ray Cooney, and after reading the script I couldn't turn it down. Luckily it was being shot in London so I could return home each evening and it was over in three weeks, but it was still full-on every day with no weekends off.

I made sure I worked really hard during those three weeks, knowing that I'd have plenty of time to spend with Betsy once filming had wrapped. But sometimes these things can drag on and decisions get made on set along the lines of: 'Let's wrap early today and shoot that part tomorrow.' Well not any more, people – hell hath no fury like a new mum being kept from her family. I was like: 'Actually, how about we stay here until midnight if necessary so I can go home and give Betsy her breakfast in the morning?!' Luckily the crew were very understanding and many had children of their own so would do their best to keep my filming on schedule.

Leaving Betsy, feeling guilty and being criticised are things I have had to get used to and I now accept it comes with the territory. Lee struggles with it too. His career had been steadily building since he won the reality TV show *Any Dream Will Do* back in 2007, and he began worrying about the time he was working and not spending with Betsy. He then started worrying that he might be offered a great job that would mean he'd need to travel and be away from Betsy even more. I reassured him that there are plenty of dads who don't get to see their children very often and we'd cross that bridge if and when we came to it. I'm sure it's something that comes with becoming a new parent – you have to find something to stress about.

Someone much more experienced in motherhood than I once told me that a mother feels guilty whatever she chooses to do and it never goes away. I have friends who spend the whole day with their baby and they feel bad because they haven't done anything else. I'll go out to work and come home to hear about all the exciting things Betsy has done while I've been away and feel guilty myself. Whatever you do, you can't win. There was one particular occasion where I noticed my mum was looking a bit down in the dumps while we were chatting so I asked her what was wrong. It turned out that having seen all the fun places I take Betsy (the playgroups and trips to the park), she wished she had done more things with me when I was younger. I guess the guilt never goes away, even once your little one has grown up and fled the nest!

A word from my Twitter followers

Steph, mum of two daughters

I was working in a senior management role when I fell pregnant with my first daughter. I was expected to take calls from my employer from my hospital bed while recovering from a Caesarean. It seems absurd when I think about it now but at the time I did it and didn't complain! I went back to work a sixty-hour week when my daughter was twelve weeks old because I thought it was what I had to do to keep my job. I soon became anxious trying to juggle a career with being a new mother and it all got too much. Twelve weeks after I returned to work I had a breakdown and was diagnosed with postnatal depression. The most important job to me is being a mummy and I am happy to say I have found a good balance now and run my own business alongside raising my two girls.

Hayley, mum to a six-month-old son

I returned to work when my beautiful baby boy was only five months old. I got fed up with people telling me how shocked they were that I was only taking six months' maternity leave and not the full year. I felt like I was being judged and made to feel guilty. My hubby and I want the best for Harry – holidays each year, nice clothes, enough money for outings etc – so returning to work was the only way we could afford it.

Alexandra, mum of two

I have my own business so only stopped working the day before I had my first baby and went back two days later. I never got to have the luxury of maternity leave and had to take my baby to work with me. I used to have her in a papoose whilst typing on the computer and would keep my fingers crossed she wouldn't scream when I answered the phone. When I had my second, two years later, I had a fortnight off work but had to take him in with me just the same after that. We all have to do what it takes to make sure we can provide for our babies.

Kelly, mum to a three-year-old daughter

I work in a predominantly male environment and when I fell pregnant with my first child everything was made difficult for me. I decided to have six months' maternity leave but ended up only having five because I kept receiving calls from work asking me to cover people's holidays. Before I returned properly I inquired whether it would be possible to go part-time or have flexible hours, which the company do offer, but my manager told me not to bother putting in for it as it would be refused. So I had no choice but to return to work six days a week. If I took my daughter for a check-up I would have to make up the time I'd missed. Last year I found out I was pregnant again. When I told my boss I was greeted with, 'What again? What are you doing to me?' This time round I have done my research and I know what I am entitled to. I can't tell you how much I'm looking forward to starting my maternity leave!

Janine, mum of two

Going back to work was brilliant: a handbag that contained only my things, a lunchtime spent reading a whole magazine and eating an undisturbed sandwich, stilettos instead of practical pram-pushing pumps and adult conversation. But hand-in-hand with that came an ache in my heart at missing my son's first pre-school sports day and a guilt that somehow wouldn't shift…

Nikki, mum of two sons

I was diagnosed with severe PND after my second son was born. As my year's maternity leave came to an end the thought of returning to work filled me with dread. I felt guilty that I'd been ill for so long and just as my children were getting their 'normal' mummy back I was abandoning them. As it turned out, going back to work was the best thing I could have done. It has given me something to focus on and makes me appreciate the time I do spend with my boys all the more.

Jen, mum to a two-year-old son

I managed to negotiate a four-day week when I returned to work but as soon as my son goes to bed, I continue to work to prove that I can get everything done. It's tough but I love the balance of spending precious time with my son.

Chapter 7

Zs for Betsy and Me

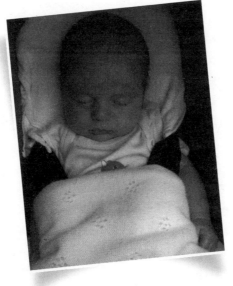

I love – and I mean L-O-V-E – my sleep. In fact, I'd go so far as to say my bed is my favourite place in the world (and could be improved only by moving it to a South Pacific island). Before Betsy came along I could sleep from 11 pm until 10 am no problem whatsoever. In fact my love of sleep has got me into trouble a few times. There was one occasion when I was fifteen and I had landed a role in the musical *Stop the World I Want to Get Off*, which was playing in London's West End. Even though I'd previously appeared in *Les Misérables* as part of the chorus, this role was my first proper part and I was so excited. The night before the show opened the cast went to a restaurant in central London to reward ourselves for all the hard work we'd been putting in. It was guaranteed to be a late night, so the owner of the stage school I attended, Sylvia Young, who was more like a mother figure to the students, very kindly allowed me to stay over at her house. This would save me having to travel back to Essex only to return to central London the next morning.

All well and good – but then I didn't turn up at the theatre the following day at 4 pm for the final rundown and vocal warm-up. Concerned, the stage manager called Sylvia to see if she knew where I was. She came into the bedroom I'd stayed in to see if I was there and left at first, thinking the bed was empty. It was only when the stage manager called again that she double-checked and found me under the covers – I was a skinny beanpole back then so the duvet must have looked like it was lying flat. I had slept for sixteen hours! It was now 5 pm, which meant I had just two and a half hours before curtain call. Luckily I made it to the theatre in record time and the show went on – I would have been mortified if I'd have missed it. Thankfully everyone saw the funny side to my little mishap so I didn't get a telling-off. The funny thing is that despite my mammoth sleep I still felt shattered and could have quite easily gone back to bed and slept for another sixteen hours.

You get the picture: when it comes to sleep I'll take it morning, noon and night – whenever, however I can get it. So when my mates who have had children, family members and even near-strangers I bumped into in the street kept telling me during my pregnancy to make the most of my sleep and enjoy the lie-ins while I could, I was a little worried. The last time I pulled an all-nighter was with my mate Tamara in Majorca the summer before I got pregnant – and I had had vodka tonics and a pumping bassline to get me through. Somehow, something told me that changing nappies and making up bottles wouldn't have the same effect!

So how on earth was I going to cope with hardly any sleep? *Would* I cope? Or would my body just run out of steam? Well, I did at least try to take the advice on board and banked a few early nights as my due date approached. But let's face it, you hardly have the most restful night's sleep towards the end of your pregnancy, what with the regular hot flushes, hourly loo trips and a ginormous belly to contend with. Plus the last thing I wanted to do was lie in bed when there were nappies to buy, pretty outfits to hang and finishing touches to the nursery to be made.

Once Betsy had arrived, my first night with her was actually not as sleepless as I'd been expecting. She woke up every couple of hours for a feed, a quick wind and cuddle before going straight back to sleep again. Making her grand entrance into the world must have worn her out nearly as much as it did me. I was both physically and emotionally exhausted from going through such a major operation and reaching the point I'd been dreaming of for the last nine months. So I was either awake tending to Betsy or out like a light – there was no in-between. In addition, I'm sure the fact that I was in hospital helped me to relax in the secure knowledge there were plenty of nurses to watch over Betsy.

While I was still in hospital I'd managed to get enough rest by grabbing precious naps whenever I could. The world of napping was all new to me as I'd never really slept during the day before – I always had a million and one things to do and usually ended up flopping into bed at night exhausted. It's the same when I'm on holiday: I could be lying in the most idyllic setting at the beginning of a week-long break and there I'd be, planning my social diary for the next few months while simultaneously devising a strategy for world peace. Now, though, grabbing a quick nap whenever I could was clearly the way forward. I'd often wake up as Betsy squeaked, gurgled or let out some noisy wind (she definitely takes after her dad in that department), but soon drifted back off again.

Lee was great and would look after Betsy when he wasn't working, allowing me to snooze safe in the knowledge that Daddy was on watch. But he couldn't always be there and, as luck would have it, he was away on the fourth night, which was a particularly hard one. Betsy cried continually all night and there was nothing I could do to comfort her. I checked her nappy, fed her, cuddled her and her temperature was fine. Still she bawled. I sat holding Betsy and feeling helpless, and as I watched the hours pass I started to panic. Perhaps this was a sign of things to come and I'd end up going crazy due to sleep deprivation!

It's amazing how over-dramatic I can be when tired. It reminded me of back in 2001 when I split up with Jay Kay and suffered with insomnia for almost a whole year as a result. I used to dread going to bed, as it was the same thing every night. I'd feel tired around late afternoon and then later as I was brushing my teeth I'd start to panic and hear a little voice saying, 'There's no point in going to bed, you're not going to be able to sleep.' I tried everything – sleeping tablets, counting sheep, meditating, hot baths, camomile tea, you name it – but nothing helped. It was awful.

Thankfully as I was still in hospital I had the nurses to reassure me that it's normal for babies to cry during the night sometimes and indeed the following night she was back to her little routine of waking up to be fed and then going straight back to sleep. Phew, it was just a blip.

One in the Bed

The first night of having Betsy at home was amazing. As I've mentioned, we'd already decided that I would sleep in the nursery with Betsy for the first six months to allow Lee to get a long stretch of sleep and then he would get up early, allowing me to lie in for a couple of hours until it was feed time again. That way in theory neither of us would be too sleep-deprived. We were very lucky to have a large spare room with a super-comfy double bed, which we'd turned into Betsy's nursery, so I positioned her Moses basket right next to me. This meant I could watch her without having to stretch too far. It was strange at first not to be curled up next to Lee but we both knew it was only short-term and the best thing for our sanity and to ensure that Lee performed well in his show. Needless to say, it took me a fair while to get to sleep as I lay there gooey-eyed, just watching her.

For the majority of the first two weeks getting enough sleep wasn't a problem. As I was stuck at home due to all the builders and scaffolding surrounding my flat, my curtains were closed the whole time and Betsy was making the most of it. In fact she did little else but sleep, so if I'd adhered to the sleep advice my mummy mates gave me, which was sleep when baby sleeps, I'd have been sleeping for eighteen hours a day. As I said, I love my sleep – but even I'd be hard-pushed to snooze for that long.

Instead, as Madam recovered from her strenuous minutes spent awake, I'd sit watching her, willing her to do something exciting, like move a finger. I'd often talk to her too and tell her how much she means to me – we've all done it, let's be honest. There would also be times where Lee and I would be in fits of giggles after our angelic daughter had produced a rather unladylike sound from her bottom, desperately trying not to laugh too loud so we didn't disturb her. I'm sure I have a video on my phone of Betsy making windy noises along with funny faces, which will come in handy when she reaches eighteen.

Unfortunately, the sleepathon didn't last long and, just a few weeks in, the long snoozes were a thing of the past. It was then that I realised the importance of the 'sleep when baby sleeps' advice. Betsy seemed to become super-sensitive to noise and light, pretty much needing silence to drift off. I watched with envy while friends would get their babies off to sleep with the TV on and the family chattering away in the same room, but no matter what I did, Betsy just didn't seem to be able to get used to background noise. I wonder if that's a hereditary trait because I've always been the same. Talk about killing the atmosphere: we'd have the TV on so low we could barely hear it for fear of disturbing her, and me being the protective mum I would snap at Lee if he spoke any louder than a whisper. The curtains would be drawn too, and we would dim the lights so low we could only just about see what we were doing.

Thankfully it didn't last too long and three to four weeks later, once we knew exactly what we could get away with without disturbing Betsy, she actually became a really good sleeper. By the age of three and a half months she was sleeping through the night – it was wonderful. I was so surprised the first night she did it when I woke up and looked at my watch. I moved her to her cot when she was twelve weeks old as she was growing out of the basket – she looked tiny in it, like a little doll! For a while it really felt like we had the dream baby. But once again, we spoke too soon.

Betsy started the early stage of teething at four and a half months and then it all went a little bit noisy. She went from sleeping from 7 pm pretty much through the night with the exception of a dream feed at 11 pm, to waking up sometimes every hour and crying inconsolably. As a new parent all you want to do is cuddle your little one back to sleep but unfortunately that doesn't solve the problem with teething. It was like being tortured: just when we thought she was settled and would start drifting off to sleep, she'd cry again. Lee and I had agreed to take it in turns to comfort Betsy as we were both working at the time and equally needed our sleep but there were a few heated discussions over whose turn it was in the early hours.

I moved out of Betsy's nursery and back into my own bed when she reached six months old. I believe there is no right and wrong with sleeping arrangements: whether you choose co-sleeping, having your baby in the same room, putting them in their own nursery or giving them a dummy to help them self-soothe – if it works for you, that's all that matters. My friend Jess put her little boy in his own nursery from the very first night and slept in the next room. She's a light sleeper and knew she would wake up at every little noise and movement Beau made if she slept in the same room. She told me a few of her friends found her decision strange but it obviously worked for her and meant she wasn't permanently exhausted during the days. I have another friend who has never set a bedtime for her kids and they have just gone to bed when they want to. Now they are at school she still just leaves them to it. She says if they are tired at school they'll learn that they need to go to bed earlier. In the end you have to follow your instincts and do what's right for you.

You also have to take into account that every child is different. My friend Cockney Vik's daughter Annabelle is four years old and has only just started sleeping through recently. She wakes up most nights wanting to play. Yet Vik also has a ten-month-old who sleeps straight through the night no problem. Some little ones just seem to find it easier to sleep than others.

I was surprised just how smoothly our sleeping transition went when I moved out of Betsy's nursery. I had been expecting a couple of difficult nights at least. But Betsy didn't even seem to notice I wasn't there, I guess because she was in the same environment. It was me who missed being in the same room as her and hearing her breathe. Mind you, I did enjoy not waking up at every tiny noise and it was nice to cuddle up to Lee again. Lee had missed our cuddles too but hadn't missed me warming my cold feet up on his legs quite so much!

Losing My Marbles

Since becoming a mum I've felt fatigue to a point I never thought possible. I've literally been so tired that it was almost painful to be awake. For the majority of the first few months I felt like I was in a bubble and would find myself doing the daftest things due to sheer sleep deprivation. I remember one occasion when I went into my local supermarket and spent ages filling my basket with everything I needed, and queuing for five minutes or so to pay, only to walk out of the shop afterwards leaving it all behind. I felt so embarrassed when I returned to see the cashier grinning from ear to ear. I can't even tell you how many times I locked myself out of my flat during the early days. My neighbour now has a spare set of keys to avoid me sitting on the doorstep blubbing my eyes out in frustration again. I've left home without Betsy's changing bag a few times and on one occasion found myself in the really awkward situation of having to come up with a makeshift nappy in the back of the car in a layby – thankfully a muslin stuffed with cotton wool worked a treat until we got home. All this forgetfulness has made me quite panicky at times, as I like to feel like I'm in control. I know I've said it before – we all have – but having a baby really is a steep learning curve.

When it gets that bad there's only one thing to do and that's to bank some sleep. One of my favourite ways is to tell Lee how knackered I am before bed and then even if I hear Betsy in the night I'll fake being asleep so Lee will have to get up. Lee's very doting anyway so he has no problem doing his share, but he has caught me out a few times and was understandably a bit miffed. The other way is to escape for a day or two from time to time, which I did recently with my friend Natalie. We went for a girly weekend to let our hair down while Lee looked after Betsy – but all I did was sleep. Bless her, she was up for boozing and chatting into the night like we've done many times over the years, but my priority was to get ten hours of uninterrupted sleep! I'm sure she'll understand when she becomes a mum as she's pregnant at the moment. It's important to get a break if you can, even if it's just for an evening at a friend's house, and if you're lucky enough to have someone to look after your little one then you can spend the night away as a couple. It's such a good way to recharge your batteries.

To Routine or Not to Routine?

I read loads on the importance of getting into a routine while I was pregnant. I read the Queen of Routine Gina Ford's book from cover to cover, as I found it so fascinating. It tells you the exact times you should wake your baby, feed them and put them down for naps in a dimly lit nursery – it even tells you when you should eat yourself. Personally I found the whole method too regimented for my lifestyle. I also got plenty of advice from friends and family on what worked for them. Mum's advice was simple: 'We didn't have all these books in my day so you had to go with what felt natural.' However one friend swore by her strict schedule – waking her little one up and feeding him by 7 am, then feeding every four hours on the dot for the rest of the day – and put the fact that her child was so angelic down to her routine being so rigid from the word go.

It was all a bit confusing and daunting so Lee and I decided to go for a middle ground and just follow an evening routine, with the aim of getting Betsy into a restful sleep pattern. We decided she would have her last bottle at the same time every afternoon followed by an hour to wind down before bath time, a bedtime story and then sleep. Easy, right?

Well, not really. It wasn't until we tried to introduce some structure that we realised how non-conformist our lives actually were. At first it seemed to throw us into all kinds of turmoil to have to stick to exact bath and bed times each evening when we had friends over or we were out and about. But we stuck with it and were soon rewarded with a tired little girl at the end of each day who couldn't wait to go to sleep. The funny thing is, I think it helps me wind down at the end of the day as well. As soon as Betsy is asleep I walk out of her bedroom, put her toys away and it's my cue to relax.

Although on the whole I can safely say that we've benefited from the bedtime routine – and certainly it helped Feni that we had established good sleep habits when she put Betsy down – I think you have to remain flexible to a degree for your own sanity. When Betsy was around seven months old, I went out for a nice afternoon coffee with friends. It was such a lovely afternoon, but then I remember looking at my watch and noticing it was getting close to Betsy's bedtime – and I started to get so stressed that we weren't in the right place at the right time that I swear I spent the last half hour not listening to a word my friends were saying, before rushing off as though my house was on fire! It was only when I got home and put Betsy to bed that I chilled out a bit and wondered what the hell I was so worried about. Betsy's far more likely to pick up on me being stressed than being half an hour late to bed.

I remember chatting to a couple who were firm believers in the whole routine thing – breakfast, lunch and dinner at the exact same time every day – who on one occasion were travelling to the coast for a short break. But they'd got caught up at home and were an hour late for leaving, so they decided to postpone the entire journey by a day because they were so worried about upsetting the daily schedule for their little one! That's a little too strict for me, maybe because of my lifestyle, but I just think routines should be more about guidelines than strict rules.

The way I see it, the decision to routine or not to routine is really more about what suits you and your lifestyle rather than what is 'best' for the baby. Your little one will be happy if you're happy, so if drawing up a spreadsheet is really your thing, then do it. Equally if you're more of a 'go with the flow' sort of person, then your baby will adapt. As ever, follow those instincts!

Catnaps

When I returned from Peru and started *Legally Blonde* in October it was nose to the grindstone and there was no room for a fuzzy head – learning lines and dance routines can take a fair amount of concentration. I've always found performing in a West End show really uplifting and I tend to be buzzing for at least an hour or two after coming off stage so I'd rarely get to bed until 1 am Unfortunately, Betsy's body clock was set to wake up between 6 and 7 am and there was no tempting her back into bed after that time (and trust me, I've tried!). So, desperate to keep on top of my sleep, I came up with a cunning plan. I became a proud owner of a little pop-up bed. I set it up in my dressing room at the theatre and became queen of the catnaps, stocking up on important Z's during the interval (when I was really desperate) and between shows on matinée day. I was so rock 'n' roll – not. Ten years ago during my hedonistic heyday, if someone had told me this is how I'd be in my mid-thirties I'd have had them sectioned!

I have had a couple of close shaves, though – almost missing cues, or stepping out on stage with bed-head and stray eyelashes. My handmade 'Do Not Disturb' sign on my door gave the game away and it wasn't long before my snoozes were common knowledge amongst the cast. One of the guys in the show, Stefan, had just had a little one too so I did the decent thing and offered him seconds on the pop-up while I was on stage. In the end we became really good at alternating our 'Nana naps', as we called them. The rest of the cast tried to get in on the act but I had a strict new-parents-only policy. Can you imagine the headline? 'Van Outen caught up in backstage bed-hopping!'

Positive Mental Attitude

I love what I do for a living and feel very lucky to get to work with such fantastic people, so despite feeling knackered I was determined to enjoy every second on stage and not moan about being tired when I reached the theatre each day. I'd often use the time it took me to travel to the theatre to think back to my time in Peru with the amazing women on the trek and I would just have an overwhelming feeling of how lucky I was to have such a beautiful family and be working as part of something as successful as *Legally Blonde*. The girls in the show were always asking for updates on Betsy so when I'd tell them I'd been up a few times in the night they'd point out that they would never hear me complain about feeling tired, but like I said to them at the time, if I was to moan it would make me ungrateful for all the positives in my life.

Of course that's very different from opening up and divulging how you feel to close friends. We all need someone to vent to sometimes and luckily I've got a strong group of girlfriends who I can turn to for advice or a sympathetic ear whenever I need to. I know they'll not only listen without making judgements but will offer impartial views as well, and if they think I'm wrong they'll certainly tell me. It's so important to have some kind of an outlet so you can express yourself if you feel like you're going crazy from sleep-deprivation. Keeping things to yourself can drive you mad and make matters feel ten times worse – especially when you're going through such an emotional and hormonally unbalanced time as early motherhood! Try to talk to a friend or family member if you can, but if you don't have them around contact your midwife or doctor. If they can't help, they'll be able to put you in touch with some support groups. There is always someone who will listen and give you the advice you need.

Thankfully the sleepless nights have decreased as Betsy's got older although I still get nights now where Betsy is up two or three times and I'll end up patting her on the back to send her back to sleep. She usually wakes up because she's dreaming and as I'm patting her she'll be singing the theme tune to the TV show *In the Night Garden*. I love hearing her sing but 'Iggy Piggle Iggle Piggle Woo!' at four in the morning I could do without.

A word from my Twitter followers

Jaimie, mum to a three-year-old daughter

When my little girl was just a few weeks old my sleep deprivation was so bad that I squirted hand soap on my toothbrush instead of toothpaste. Needless to say, it didn't taste very nice.

Melissa, mum to a six-year-old son

When my little boy Marley was born he was a little monkey when it came to sleeping in his Moses basket. He just didn't like it, so it was fun and games in the middle of the night after feeding him to get him to go back down. My husband and I came up with a plan – when I got Marley out to feed him my husband would put the top I had worn that day in his Moses basket and put a hot water bottle in there too. Then, when I had finished feeding we took the hot water bottle out and put Marley back in. That way he went from something warm and mummy-smelling to something warm and mummy-smelling! It worked a treat and we never had any problems getting him to sleep in his Moses again.

Kirsty, mum of two daughters

When my eldest daughter was just a few weeks old she woke me up in the early hours to let me know she had done a little present in her nappy. After I'd changed her she gave me the biggest smile, which melted my heart, so I grinned back and said, 'Oh baby, you're so gorgeous.' That was it! She thought it was playtime and was awake for hours. By the time my second bundle of joy came along I had learned my lesson and no matter how much she smiles I don't say a word.

Joanne, mum of two sons

I had trouble getting my son to sleep when he was a few weeks old. Then one day I was watching MTV when Dido's 'White Flag' came on. Reece stopped crying and had fallen asleep by the end of the song. From then on I would play the song whenever I wanted him to sleep and it worked every time. Five years later, my youngest son Jake does the same to Will Young's 'Leave Right Now'. Grandma has even learned the words so she can sing it to him.

Eleanor, mum to two-year-old twin boys

The best piece of advice I have for any mum, but especially a mum of twins, is to get into a good routine for feeding and sleeping. You want your twins to do things at the same time so you get some downtime for yourself for that cup of tea or a nap. It also pays to plan ahead – I made lots of meals for me and my hubby before the boys were born so on days when I couldn't muster up the energy to cook we had a nice nutritious meal to grab out of the freezer and pop in the microwave.

Sarah, mum of two

I had a hard time of it when my son was born. He never slept and I'm convinced it was because I was a panicky first-time mum. When my daughter came along I was determined she would sleep. I would get her out of her crib at 10 pm and breastfeed her while she was still half-asleep then put her back down. She slept through the night from three weeks old!

Claire, mum of three sons

I have read to my three boys at bedtime since they were tiny. It quickly became part of their routine and helped to settle them so they can sleep. My youngest is now two – he fetches his book and says, 'Bedtime, Mummy!'

Lisa, mum of three daughters

We struggled to get all three of our girls to sleep until we introduced a regular routine. We would bath them in Sleepytime bubble bath, let them have one last play in the water, dry them in a warm room with dim lighting, feed them some warm milk, sing them a lullaby and it was off to bed. As soon as we had established the routine they slept for twelve to fourteen hours a night!

Eliza, mum to a four-year-old

The best way to get a baby who is over three months to sleep is to follow a basic bath and bedtime routine. Then once in the cot, pop a blanket over your baby or a little rolled-up towel either side like a buffer, which will make them feel secure. Make sure the light is low and there aren't any toys around to distract them. Leave them to get themselves off to sleep. If they cry for more than a few minutes go into them, stroke them and reassure them – but don't pick them up! It's hard but that's the key. Each night your baby will cry for a shorter time. They aren't scared and confused as they can be when the crying-out method is used. It really works. Once they settle you can go and have that glass of wine you really deserve!

Kate, mum to a five-year-old daughter

My daughter was born at twenty-nine weeks which was horrific at the time but luckily we now have a beautiful, healthy five-year-old. I picked up some great tips during our time in the baby unit. One of them is useful if your baby tends to bring their milk up after a feed. Place a small, soft hand towel on top of baby's sheet and any milk will soak into the towel and you won't need to change the sheets quite as often.

Chapter 8

Two Become Three

Having a baby is a double-edged sword. On the one hand it's the biggest commitment you and your other half will make to each other, but on the other it places a massive strain on a relationship. I knew (or thought I knew) that everything that comes with a new baby – the tiredness, lack of time for each other and resulting breakdown in communication – adds pressure on a relationship, but even I wasn't fully prepared for it. And I have to say, it's hardly surprising that a lot of relationships run into difficulty as soon as a baby comes along. It's the first (and probably only) time in your relationship when you are living very separate lives – you're jealous of him for the fact that his life has barely changed, and he still gets to be his own person, while he's jealous of you for getting to stay at home all day when he's knackered and has to go off to work.

One thing I hadn't taken into consideration before becoming a mum was that I would find myself thinking about Betsy morning, noon and night, leaving little time to dwell on anything or anyone else. Don't get me wrong, it's lovely to always have her in my thoughts, but it has led to problems at times. Lee has pointed out on numerous occasions that after Betsy was born the only time we spoke to one another was to relay the latest on Betsy. Our usual handover would be along the lines of: 'She's just been fed, had a dirty nappy and is due for a sleep soon.' Lee was right when he complained that I rarely asked him how his day had gone before bombarding him with a list of instructions for Betsy. To be fair though, I had nothing else going on in my life so whereas before we'd chat naturally with each other about what we'd both been up to at work, my day was now all about looking after Betsy. Often when Lee and I finally found an opportunity to talk last thing at night in bed he would stop mid-sentence and ask whether I'd listened to a word he had said. I must admit that at times his voice was little more than background noise as I ran through Betsy's schedule for the following day in my head or listened out for the monitor in case she was stirring. Of course this would lead to words and occasionally an argument.

It hasn't helped that once Betsy got a little older we were both balancing being parents with going out to work. There have been times where we've both had roles in musicals so we've rarely had time together in the evenings once Betsy is asleep and the chaos of the day has subsided. We do of course try to find time in the day to spend together but it's far from romantic – when we're not looking after Betsy, we're usually doing something practical like arranging insurance renewals or paying bills. I'd be lying if I said it didn't take its toll on our relationship and there have been times when Lee and I have taken it out on one another. Of course I am always right and Lee is in the wrong – hee hee!

First Family Outing

One of the most important things to do to keep your relationship healthy when a baby arrives is to make time for outings together as a family. This can feel very strange at first as obviously your roles are now different and even if you return to one of your favourite pre-pregnancy haunts you'll find nothing is the same with a baby in tow. But it's part of adjusting to life together as a new family unit so it's worth making the effort to get out.

Betsy was two months old when we decided to have our first lunch out together as a family. Lee and I love our Sunday roasts – and before we had Betsy one of our favourite things was to take a trip to our local pub for some good old-fashioned pub grub before collapsing on the sofa in a food coma. So it seemed fitting that our first family outing was … drum roll … for a roast!

We'd been going to this same pub for a few years now so had witnessed our fair share of mayhem as families took on the Sunday ritual together – mums and dads trying to read the papers while the kids ripped the pages, threw food on the floor and banged the tables with anything they could get their mitts on. I have to admit to sniggering now and then as the little ones did everything they could to cause disruption – and laughing as, despite all this, their parents seemed to remain defiantly calm and relaxed. Maybe it's a

Sunday thing as someone else was cooking! But now that it was our turn to experience the parental perspective, I was hoping it wasn't payback time.

Betsy was still very little so we were safe in the knowledge that there wouldn't be any food flung on the floor but I couldn't help but feel anxious as we stood outside the pub with Madam in the buggy. I was dreading weaving through the tables trying desperately not to knock a bottle of wine into someone's lap. Do all mums play out dramas in their heads before anything has even happened, or is it just me? Anyway, as usual all the worrying was for nothing as Lee safely led the way to a table in a quiet corner. The staff were as welcoming as always and took the time to come over to meet her ladyship. Many of them had witnessed me grow steadily throughout my pregnancy and had been fabulously accommodating, especially when it came to my weird and wonderful food requests (pickled gherkin anyone?), so it was great for them to finally meet Betsy.

I felt so proud as everyone cooed over her telling me how gorgeous she was. Betsy was less impressed by the meet-and-greet and barely opened her eyes for the whole afternoon, which gave Lee and I plenty of time to enjoy our delicious food and to chat to each other.

Having Lee with me for moral support gave me the confidence to venture to the toilet to change Betsy's nappy. Up until then I had only attempted this on the change table in her nursery so it was a big deal for me. Unfortunately the change table was in the ladies' loo (as is often the case), which meant Lee couldn't actually come in with me to lend a helping hand. I had a little panic as I looked around for somewhere to hang the change bag while keeping a firm hand on Betsy's tummy. To make matters worse the sensor-activated hand dryer was right next to the change table and kept going off, scaring the life out of us both. Dramas aside, I managed to successfully complete the job and get us safely back to the security of our table.

Whereas we would have normally flicked through the papers, Lee and I spent most of our time catching up with each other over a cheeky glass of red and gazing at our little angel. I felt the effects of the wine pretty much straight away as it was only the second time I had drunk alcohol in months and in any case I'm a complete lightweight when it comes to drinking during the day. It was a lovely way to spend the afternoon and to top it off when we got back to the flat we all curled up on the sofa and had an afternoon nap – bliss!

Needless to say the tradition continues – we've been back countless times as Betsy has grown. It's not quite so smooth sailing now as she throws tons of food all over the floor, but makes up for it by waving to all the staff to soften them up (a little trick I find works when I'm on a boozy night out). I think she might even see the pub as an extension of her playgroup now.

Time for Each Other

As well as days out as a family, of course, you also need to remember you and your partner's own relationship as a couple. This is not as easy as it sounds. An invaluable piece of advice I received from a fabulous mum of four is to regularly stop what you're doing to consider whether you are finding enough time for your partner. Whenever I did that I realised Lee and I definitely weren't finding enough, if any, time for one another – let alone time to be intimate. You need to make an effort, which I found really hard.

On one occasion when Betsy was four months old, Lee asked my mum if she would mind looking after her so he could surprise me with a romantic night out. Somehow I got wind of what he was planning but instead of feeling excited about the prospect of going out, I just felt it was the last thing I wanted to do as I was so exhausted. I told Lee that I'd rather catch up on sleep instead and that caused another argument. Once we had calmed down we talked about how we were both feeling and promised each other we would work to get things back on track. We began putting dates in our diaries to spend the evening together as a couple, whether it was a trip to the cinema or a romantic dinner. It may sound a bit weird (I was once told about a certain famous couple who communicated with each other via their PAs – now *that's* bizarre) but we found that if we didn't put a date in our diaries parenthood would take over and we'd end up running around all day until we collapsed on the sofa, exhausted and unable to move.

Our nights out were really enjoyable – we looked forward to them, got dressed up and talked like we did in the early days of our relationship. It's funny because we had been so busy focusing on Betsy it almost felt as though we were getting to know each other again.

Love Life (or Lack of)

Towards the end of my pregnancy making love turned into more of an orienteering exercise than a spontaneous act of affection, and that's without even taking into account the worry of squashing the baby! I have friends who were at it like rabbits right up until their baby arrived (and good for them, they do say it's one of the things that brings on labour, after all), and they continued as their baby slept in a crib next to the bed. On the other side, I have mates who, three years on, are concerned their sex lives may never be the same. Lee and I are neither one side nor the other, but I'd question any couple who say their love life wasn't affected in some way by pregnancy and the arrival of their new baby.

Given the often-painful recovery period after giving birth, the complete rollercoaster of emotions us mums experience and the lack of sleep and change in lifestyle that all parents go through, it's really hard to motivate yourselves back to a healthy sex life once your baby bombshell has arrived. Then there's the underwear. You go from wearing sexy feminine lingerie sets (or at least matching!) to bras that could be used as slingshots and knickers that come up to the bust line. Not to mention the attractive breast pads that are a necessity to soak up any leaking milk. I mean come on, ladies, how could any man resist? Throw into the mix a career for either or both parents and getting jiggy in the sack can seem nigh on impossible. That is certainly the situation we found ourselves in.

That's not to say that as soon as Betsy came along we lost all feeling from the hips down. It was more a case of needing to schedule. For quite a while we just didn't seem to both be in the mood for romance at the same time, so we simply ended up going without for ages. At the time I wondered whether our love life would ever return to normal, but thankfully it did. A healthy sex life is an important part of a relationship, so it's something we've worked hard at to get back on track. And let's face it, it's not the worst thing in the world to work on, is it?

Daddy Time

When Betsy first came along Lee also found it pretty difficult to cope with the adjustments to our lives and sleep patterns. He was constantly exhausted from rehearsing for his show into the evenings and then still being woken up early by Betsy. There were a few weeks when he could have easily got a part as a zombie in any stage show.

Despite feeling shattered he was always fantastic with Betsy (or his little Munch as he calls her, short for munchkin). Right from the word go he spent plenty of time looking after her while we were still in hospital and became really confident around her. It was lovely to see. Of course I didn't have any doubts that he'd be a great dad but I did wonder how quickly he'd take to it. Yet from the moment Betsy arrived he seemed more patient and grown up. He's also much more driven and determined in what he wants to achieve so he can make sure Betsy has a comfortable life.

Unfortunately as his rehearsal and performance schedules became more intense he spent more time at work and less time with us. He'd dash in every night, mortified that he might have missed something. He'd ask what Betsy had been up to so I'd point to her all snug and sleepy in her Moses basket and say, 'That!' Despite my attempts to convince him he wasn't missing anything he was still upset he wasn't around more. Also, because he wasn't as hands-on as before, he lost a bit of confidence around her, something that I know a lot of new dads have trouble with.

In this situation it's natural for the mother to take over a lot of the responsibilities in a kind of default way and that's exactly what I did for a while. But we felt it was really important for Lee to be as hands-on as possible, so with a little helpful advice from my mum I just learned to bite my tongue every time he was taking an age to change Betsy's nappy or if he was holding her in a way I wouldn't. Gradually he found his feet again.

When I went to Peru for the trek he spent the whole week looking after Betsy. I returned expecting the place to be a bombshell and to find Lee tearing his hair out – but actually the flat was spick and span and Lee was on a high from his week with his Munch. Bless him, he'd kept up a busy social diary too: they'd been to the zoo, the park and visited friends. There were plenty of pictures to update me on their adventures, which were lovely to see – despite the fact Lee had dressed Betsy in the most uncoordinated, ridiculous outfits each day (why do dads do this?)! She looked happy, so I just let that one go.

Now Betsy is older she loves to run around and play hide-and-seek with her daddy – and I love to see them having so much fun together. Although when Lee puts Betsy on his shoulders, which is her favourite place to be, I'm a nervous wreck until her feet are safely back on solid ground. He really is a wonderful dad. Betsy's a lucky girl and I'm extremely lucky too.

A word from my Twitter followers

Tina, mum of two

I have a theory that having a baby will downgrade your relationship for up to a year after you give birth. If you have a brilliant relationship it will become OK, an OK one will become dodgy, and a dodgy one is on seriously dangerous ground. I was petrified when I became pregnant with my second child because I knew how bad it had become between my husband and I the first time round. A few months after the birth we had even discussed divorce – this was literally one of the lowest points in my life. Thankfully though, I think if you can make it through that bad patch you actually end up stronger. On the days when the kids are 'challenging', my husband and I unite, and it almost feels a bit like it's 'us v them'. And on the days when everyone is behaving we have a magical, secure little family!

Donna, mum to a two-year-old son

My partner and I had only been together for six months when I fell pregnant and the relationship has been in turmoil since I gave birth to our son. Alfie was a week old when the blazing rows started and we have probably split up twenty times since. Our sex life has been non-existent since the birth, as I've totally lost my sex drive, whereas my partner's seems to have increased, which gives us plenty to argue about. Two and half years ago I was full of life, wanting to make the best of every minute with family and friends, and now I'm stuck in a relationship which is not doing either of us any good.

Clare, mum to two sons aged six months and two years

Boy, if I thought one baby had changed the dynamics of my relationship with my husband, two has nearly led us to divorce. It's made me question whether I'm neglecting my husband and the answer is a resounding 'yes'. I'm finding it tough to be a mum to two small children and fulfill my duties as a wife. All I do know is I couldn't be without him. It's so hard having two children and not having a family support network in the local area. We don't get to have date nights – our life is our children. But we wouldn't have it any other way and I'm sure once our boys are older my husband and I can get things back on track.

Emma, mum to a three-year-old

We were the first of our friends to have a baby. My partner found it difficult, as when our little one was small everything was just about feeding, changing and sleeping. Our friends weren't much help as they didn't understand how sleep-deprived you get or the financial impact a baby has on your life. My partner ended up having an affair for around a month. When I found out, he said he wanted to have something different to focus on other than babies. I decided to work through things and as our little one grew older things got better. He's now absolutely brilliant: I wouldn't want a better dad for my child and we are getting married later in the year! I'm not condoning what he did but do feel that men can be affected by having a baby. No one really warns you to look out for your relationship.

Claire, pregnant mum-to-be

I'm seven months' pregnant and even before the baby has arrived it's starting to put a strain on our relationship. Due to being so uncomfortable at night we now sleep in separate beds – he always makes out that it's OK but I know deep down it's killing him. As for our sex life, I have really lost my drive! I know it's not him as I still fancy and love him so much – I tell him every day but I do wonder if he believes me. All this is before the baby is even here and it worries me a great deal.

Samantha, mum to a one-year-old daughter

When I was twenty-one weeks' pregnant my hubby was sent for a tour of duty in Afghanistan. It broke my heart but I made a pregnancy book full of scan pics and a pic of me and our baby bump every week. He returned for two weeks when our daughter was born then back to the sandpit he went. He returned home for good eight weeks later and our relationship is as strong as ever. We have both learned that life is far too short and to cherish every moment, so why argue over the loo seat being left up or dirty cups being left in the sink? It's not worth it. As a result our love life is very good and we seize the opportunity whenever our baby is asleep. We feel that having our daughter has completed us; we couldn't be happier and we're more in love than ever. Whilst he was away the main form of contact between us was letters so we would write down all our feelings. You can't re-read a phone call but letters are there forever.

Helen, mum to a six-year-old son

My baby father and I were very much in love when we found out we were pregnant and we were over the moon. I did wonder if we were ready but my partner and his mum convinced me that we were so I spent the next few months preparing to be a mother. When I was seven months' pregnant my partner came home from work, packed his things and left. I never saw him again! I blamed my unborn child and hit rock bottom but now, six years on, I'm a single parent and I'm doing well. My son doesn't have a father figure but we are very happy and I love our little family.

Kate, mum to a six-month-old daughter

My husband and I tried for two years before discovering we could not have a baby naturally so we decided to go for ICSI treatment (advanced IVF). Our first two treatments on the NHS didn't work. You can imagine how stressful it was trying to keep positive while it seems everyone around you is getting pregnant. I got to the point where I couldn't even look at a pregnant lady. Our third treatment worked but unfortunately I had a miscarriage at eleven weeks, which sent me into more of a depression. Again our relationship became stronger and my husband and I supported each other through it with the help of my family. Finally on our fourth attempt we were blessed with a gorgeous girl, Ruby Tallulah. The whole experience has made us become a very solid partnership and I am lucky to have my soulmate.

Chapter 9

Food Glorious Food

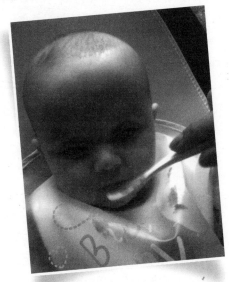

From the moment Betsy was born she had a good appetite and would always drink plenty of milk at each feed. While I was breastfeeding she gulped it down – I never had a problem with her not taking enough, it was simply that she started to refuse to latch on after I'd given her expressed milk in a bottle. And once we'd switched to formula it was unusual if we didn't hear the sucking air noise that comes from an empty bottle. In fact, the only time she wasn't really that interested in milk was when she was badly teething. Can't say I blame her: who really fancies a drink when suffering from bad toothache?

For the first three months I would watch Betsy while she fed, absolutely amazed that she was thriving and growing on nothing more than milk. It is a natural wonder how all mammals survive solely on milk until they wean and move on to solid foods (listen to me getting all Sir David Attenborough!).

I used to spend hours wondering how life would be so much easier if milk continued to provide all the nutrition we needed as adults and I could serve it up for dinner each night and not have to worry about being imaginative or doing the weekly supermarket shop. I'd just have one massive milk delivery – a whole milk float for our household. I can see it now (Lee: 'What have we got for dinner, babe?' Me: 'Milk again, lovely'). Yes, these are the crazy thoughts that fill my brain. Is 'baby brain' still a valid excuse nearly two years after giving birth?

However, it's not long before babies need something else in their diet, so suddenly the ease of milk feeds goes out the window and it's time to get creative.

To Wean or Not to Wean?

As Betsy approached five months she started taking an interest in what I was eating, and she'd watch with intent as I put food in my mouth. Sometimes she would appear to be pretending to put invisible food in her own mouth – the budding actress in her coming out already. That soon progressed to her reaching towards my plate as I ate my lunch and trying to help herself. Taking this as a sure sign she wanted something other than milk, I turned to my encyclopaedic collection of baby books to look for advice. What I found was very confusing. The majority of books these days recommend that the weaning process is started around the six-month mark, but when I was a baby the average age was three months. My mum started weaning me when I was four months. I wasn't sure what to do!

Despite what I'd read, once again it was my friends and family who proved to be more useful in helping me make the decision as to when the right time was to start weaning Betsy. I was doing a photo shoot for a magazine with Fearne Cotton and got chatting to her stylist, Sinead, who has a little one six months older than Betsy. We had covered pretty much every baby-related topic (much to poor Fearne's dismay, as she was thoroughly bored with all the baby talk), when we got on to weaning. I filled her in on my dilemma and she told me she too had found the whole thing confusing and in the end she just did what intuitively felt right. She advised me to trust my own instincts, and if Betsy was showing the typical signs of being ready for food (she was almost eating her own hand!) then I should go for it. That was obviously what I needed to hear as I made the decision then and there: weaning would commence.

I found the thought of giving Betsy anything other than milk really scary. I'd heard and read so many horror stories about babies choking. My friend Karen knows just how terrifying it can be to experience a choking incident. When her daughter Rose was eight months old she was eating banana for the first time when it got lodged in her throat. Rose started coughing and turned from a normal healthy colour through red to an almost purple shade within a matter of moments. For a couple of seconds

Karen froze before her natural instinct kicked in – which I find fascinating – and she grabbed Rose out of her highchair, turned her upside-down and patted her firmly on the back until she dislodged the banana. I'll never forget the phone call I received from Karen that afternoon to say she was in A&E getting Rose checked out. Even though Rose was fine by then, Karen was horrified by the 'What if...?' By the end of the conversation we had decided to take a first-aid course together, so if anything like that should ever occur again with Rose or Betsy we would be well-prepared for it. We managed to get a few of our mummy mates together round at Karen's house and split the cost of the two-hour course with a qualified first-aider. In the end it cost me £20 – a small price to pay for peace of mind.

Let the Fun Commence

The day before I gave Betsy her first yummy mush I re-read all the relevant chapters in my various books on weaning and the leaflets I had been given during my first-aid course to make sure I knew exactly what to do if Betsy was to ever get food stuck in her throat. Slightly over-cautious perhaps, bearing in mind the first food for a baby is barely even pulp, but I was so worried after the incident with Rose I wasn't taking any chances.

First up was baby rice. With Lee on hand for a bit of moral support and with his camera at the ready to witness the important milestone, I prepared Betsy's first real food and sat her in the high chair for the first time. As she tasted her first mouthful she had an inquisitive look on her face before making what can only be described as a noise of approval and contentment. A couple of spoonfuls later and she couldn't get enough. I'd prepared myself for splattered walls and maximum mess but my hungry girl was intent on eating every last drop. She just kept pushing her head forward with her mouth open like a hungry hippo. I was so pleased, as it confirmed that my instincts had been right to try her with something other than milk. A couple of days later and she was grabbing for the spoon – I obviously wasn't moving fast enough for her. I was hoping this was a sign of things to come and that we had a good eater on our hands.

The baby rice was a roaring success, so the next step was to experiment with something with a bit more flavour. Mashed sweet potato and carrots went down just as well. As I tried her with new flavours her eyebrows would raise a little followed by a wave of excitement running through her body that would have her lifting her ams and kicking her legs. I became much more confident and started to enjoy putting on my pinny and cooking up tasty treats. It became one of those jobs that made me feel like a proper mum. There were definitely days, and there still are now, when I'm feeling a bit rushed and I wish I could knock up a bottle of milk as a quick fix, but as soon as Betsy's eyes light up when she is eating, the hours (well, minutes, perhaps) I've spent slaving over a hot stove are all worth it.

I found the best way to cope with the demand for food was to wait until she was asleep and then cook up some tasty concoctions for her to try. If she liked them I'd then pop them into tiny ice cube-type pots to freeze so I could stack up about a weeks' worth ready to be defrosted when needed. Lee always felt a little hard done by as he never got anywhere near this much attention on the food front but, as I pointed out, if he's happy to eat parsnip and carrot purée then I'll happily make him a week's worth at the same time.

Don't get me wrong, though, I wasn't always perfectly prepared. I'd keep a stash of pouches to hand if ever I was caught out or we were going out for the day. Betsy was a huge fan of the Ella's Kitchen meals and loved every flavour. My favourite was the vegetable bake – it was delicious!

Looking back at the first steps of weaning I wonder why I made such a fuss. There was no way Betsy would choke on a bit of baby rice or puréed carrot, especially with me watching over her like a hawk, but when it was time to move on to proper solids I was definitely more nervous. I'm sure Betsy must have found it a bit weird the first couple of times I gave her something to hold herself and eat – I stood in front of her poised like a goalkeeper with cat-like reflexes ready to pounce at the first sign of gagging. I'd breathe a huge sigh of relief every time she'd finish a chunk of bread or rice cake without any dramas, which of course was the majority of the time.

In the following few weeks there were times when Betsy made a gagging noise and spat the offending food item out on to her tray table before I'd had the chance to whisk her from the highchair and pat her on the back. However there was one particular occasion that frightened the life out of me. We were on a flight when I gave Betsy a baby rice cake to tide her over before dinner. Before I could stop her she shoved pretty much the whole of it in her mouth and tried to swallow it without so much as a single chew. She started gagging instantly and looked at me with a deep-set panic in her eyes, which were already red around the edges and watering. I took her out of her seat and gave her a few firm taps on her back, eventually dislodging it from her throat. To anyone watching I'm sure I looked a picture of calmness but inside I was seriously panicking. It was times like that when I could literally feel my heart pounding so hard that it felt like it was about to pop out of my chest! Although it is always frightening to see your baby gagging and coughing you definitely get used to it the more often it happens.

I learned a valuable lesson round at my friend's house one lunchtime. Her daughter was fourteen months at the time and capable of feeding herself, but I watched in disbelief as she stuffed a quarter of a sandwich in her mouth and turned to her mum to gauge her reaction. I was horrified and ready to pounce but my mate just sat there as her daughter spat the whole thing back out again – it was impossible for her to chew with so much in her mouth. As my friend whispered, 'She has to learn.' And indeed, next time her daughter took a sensible-sized bite. Job done.

By the time Betsy was just over a year old she was pretty much eating baby-size portions of the same food as us, so the time came for her to experience her first Sunday roast. She'd been to our local pub plenty of times before, of course, but this would be the first time she would actually taste the delicious food herself. It's Lee and I's favourite meal of the week and we'll eat every morsel on our plate without fail, so we were hoping Betsy would enjoy it just as much. As we were about to order our food it dawned on me that it would be ridiculous for Betsy to have her own portion as they were so huge, so Lee and I decided we should each put a bit of our lunch on to a separate plate for her. There was a tense silence between

Lee and I as we waited for the food and when our meals arrived it became apparent why ... We love our daughter unconditionally but we clearly have trouble sharing our roasts, and so we were holding what can only be described as a hilarious silent argument over who should put what on the plate for Betsy! Lee was a bit miffed as to why he had ended up offering his Yorkshire pud (the holy grail of any roast dinner) when I had only popped a couple of carrots and green beans on the plate, but in our house when it's boy v girls he always loses. From then on it was decided that it would be best for Betsy to have her own meal to keep the peace, and whatever she didn't eat would be taken home in a doggie bag for our imaginary dog.

Oh, and I'm pleased to report that Betsy is definitely our daughter because she ate every last scrap.

Learn to Love the Mess

If you haven't yet experienced the mayhem of allowing your little one to feed themselves, I have two vital pieces of advice. The first is to invest in a large sheet of plastic and the other is to relax. It will get messy, that's a guarantee, so spread the plastic sheeting on the floor to cover an effective landing zone and then stand well back. There is no way a baby can have a bowl of food in front of them and a spoon in hand without some food being launched over the edge of their high chair. Worst-case scenario is that the whole bowl is going over, landing sunny-side down.

It amazes me how babies can be so amazingly accurate with their fingers when it comes to picking up the tiniest things off the floor – and whatever they pick up normally goes straight into their mouth, so there's no doubting their hand-eye coordination. However, give them a spoon and a bowl of food and it all goes out the window! The spoon goes in the bowl upside-down and side-to-side, and then straight in the hair or on to the table for the other hand to spread around, creating a work of food art right before your eyes. Of course it all happens with the brightest of grins. Babies seem to get so much pleasure in getting covered in something they know they should really be eating. There have been plenty of occasions when baby wipes haven't been enough to clean Betsy after a meal and I've ended up carrying her straight to the bathroom for a quick rinse. It's extraordinary where you find stray bits of food – round the neck, in the ears and up the nose!

Healthy Diet

It's really important to me that Betsy has a healthy diet and gets as many vitamins and minerals as possible. We're really lucky with the choices we have available in our supermarkets these days. I was given a varied diet as a child – everything came with veg and I even loved sprouts. I'm convinced that's why I love healthy food now. Of course, there are times when Betsy is offered food that is far from healthy at birthday parties or when we're visiting friends, but I'm pretty relaxed with letting her try things. I believe that if you stop a child from eating a particular food they are more likely to crave it in the future. As long as she's not having foods packed full of artificial colours or sweeteners that are harmful then I have no problem with the occasional party platter.

When I'm cooking at home, I try to make the food look tempting for Betsy. Some of the stuff you buy in jars just looks disgusting so I have a rule that if it doesn't look good or if I wouldn't eat it myself, I wouldn't feed it to Betsy. As she's got older I've started to make faces with food on her plate. I'm not sure she fully appreciates my artistic flair but it seems to keep her interested in the food, as she'll pretty much try everything. That doesn't necessarily mean she likes everything I cook: there have been times when I've slaved away in the kitchen only to receive a screwed-up face and pursed lips when I serve up my latest delicacy. I don't get stressed out though, as of course sometimes she's genuinely not hungry or is feeling unwell. My little trick is to offer her a yoghurt, which is her favourite food on the planet. If she isn't tempted then I know she's 100 per cent off her food.

As Betsy's got older I've experimented more with different tastes, textures and seasonings and gathered quite a collection of baby cookbooks. We often all sit down to a dinner based on a recipe from one of Betsy's books, and I'll just add a touch of seasoning for us. Mind you, Betsy doesn't seem to mind a bit of spice, as we found out by accident. I can laugh about it now but at the time I almost strangled Lee. I'd made two stir-fries – one for Lee and I with chillies and spices, and one for Betsy, which was chilli-free. Lee was halfway through feeding Betsy the hot one by mistake when I raced into the room, expecting to see her gasping for air and her eyes watering. Instead I was greeted by a huge smile. She couldn't get enough of it.

I feel extremely lucky that Betsy is a good little eater and I hope she continues to be. My mate Karen had a really tough time getting her daughter Rose to eat when she was two, as she would rather be running around and playing with her toys. She would do everything she could to get out of her highchair and would often not touch a single spoonful of her food. Karen was really concerned at one point but it was just a phase and thankfully Rose grew out of it.

A Positive Attitude to Food

When I was growing up we always ate together at the dining table as a family and we pretty much finished everything on our plates at each mealtime, and to be honest I think we're healthier for it. So whenever I can I always have Betsy's high chair at the table and sit to eat with her so she can see me eating and clearing my plate too. That way she tends to eat more, plus it's a nice thing to do together – an important part of being a family in my eyes.

The fact that I have a daughter has made me think a lot about how I'd like her to view food when she's older. I don't want her to be on constant diets as a teenager or, worst-case scenario, end up with an eating disorder. It may come across as a weird thing to be worrying about when she's still so young but I know better than most about the way women are portrayed in the press and the pressure it can put on developing young minds. I'm lucky that I have never suffered from an eating disorder but I have friends who have and I have witnessed how it can destroy a person's life and those around them. One of my friends told me that she is positive her problems stemmed from hearing her mum talk about diets and being fat when she was young, so I know how important my role is in shaping Betsy's attitude.

Eating Out

Eating out with a baby or toddler can be an experience in itself. The number one rule is to definitely be prepared for all eventualities. If you have everything you need – a bib, wipes, a bowl, spoons – you are halfway there. All you have to hope for is a well-behaved baby.

Betsy loves to be out and about and can get really excitable when we go out for food. She seems to love the buzz and atmosphere that comes with being in a restaurant, particularly if there are other kids in there as well. I've eaten in most of the restaurants in my local area at one time or another, but if I'm with Betsy I'll always make sure I choose a child-friendly place because I can't always guarantee that she'll be on her best behaviour. I have no problem bending under the table twenty times during a meal to pick up cutlery, crayons or fish sticks, but I hate to feel people are scowling at me. There is a great place on Hampstead High Street called Giraffe, which is part of a larger chain across the country – I'm sure you know it! They have loads of high chairs, do super-healthy food and aren't bothered if your little one makes a mess. That's definitely my kind of place to eat out with Betsy so we'll head there before anywhere else and always have a fun time.

In my opinion mealtimes are one of the areas in which you have to start exercising discipline. There is a fine line between making them fun and letting them degenerate into all-out chaos. Betsy was ten months when she took me completely by surprise, deciding to blow a mouthful of food all over me. Luckily this was at home and not in a restaurant, because no matter how child-friendly the place is I would have been absolutely mortified. Needless to say my reaction to having lamb and carrot spat over my face and jumper was quite animated and the look of shock on my face must have been an expression my little monkey hadn't seen before so, intrigued, she promptly did it again. That was it – I wasn't prepared to risk another showering so I took the plate away from her. Betsy's expression switched in an instant as she realised it wasn't a game and that she was being naughty. Her bottom lip turned downwards as she started to cry and hold her arms out for a cuddle. Of course she got a cuddle and it all calmed down, but she didn't get the plate of food back. Instead I gave her a nice ripe pear for dessert after a few minutes as a peace offering.

Bring on the terrible twos!

A word from my Twitter followers

Jodie, mum to eight-month-old twins

I am currently weaning my babies. Yesterday was the first time they had a breakfast, lunch and dinner without a bottle. I started on baby rice, which they hated, and I ended up mixing the baby rice with mashed foods. I always have a bottle made up just in case it goes wrong but have introduced foods slowly to make sure they like the flavours and different textures. It's still an ongoing process. As I have to feed two babies at once I use one bowl and one spoon and alternate the spoonfuls. I was using two bowls and two spoons at first but I was getting covered in food!

Hannah, mum of two

For my firstborn I did everything the Annabel Karmel book suggested. I would carefully purée fruit then spoon it into ice-cube trays to be frozen. For my second I started weaning at five months and bought fruit pots that I then divided up and froze in the same way. This was much less time-consuming, particularly with a three-year-old attached to your ankles!

Louise, mum of two

I am a mum of two and unusual for western society as I follow non-western methods. I nurse my children until they are self-weaned, co-sleep, use baby-led solids, nursed through pregnancy and now breastfeed in tandem with my new son and my toddler daughter, which has created a wonderful bond between them.

Amanda, mum of two

My friend and I talked at great lengths most days about when and how we would wean our babies. When it came to my second I was quite relaxed about it. Once Sadie got to about six months old, we started to give her what we were having. If she ate any, great; if she didn't, that was fine too! She was getting everything from her milk anyway and food was an added bonus so we never made a fuss about her finishing all her dinner.

Nicki, mum to a ten-month-old daughter

I have breastfed from day one and I'm still going strong now. I have baby-led weaned Isla from six months and I can't rave about it enough. I haven't pulped, puréed or mashed a single thing since she's been on solids and she is now already very capable at picking up food, chewing and swallowing. I just wanted to share this as I have found it a very humbling experience. It has shown me what truly amazing little things babies are and how quick and capable they are if we allow them to learn things for themselves.

Gemma, mum to a 21-month-old daughter

The best advice on weaning I was given was very simple: when the baby starts waking up in the night looking for food when they had previously been sleeping through, it's time to start them on solids. It worked for us!

Natalie, mum to an eleven-month-old son

We've had a great success with baby-led weaning. We used to give our son home-made purée but after eating food pouches on holiday he wouldn't go back to home-made and started to refuse to be fed with a spoon. On the advice of my breastfeeding counselling group I ordered a book on baby-led weaning and learned the theory of it first before giving it a go. The first time we tried it I cooked carrot and toast with jam, and he picked the food up with his hands and ate it! We started with food that he could mash with his hands and over time we moved on to all foods. He is ten months now and will confidently eat any food.

Karen, mum of two

When I was weaning I was really conscious of what I fed my two kids and would spend hours mushing and blending fruit and vegetables and freezing them in ice-cube trays. Sometimes it drove me round the bend and I wondered if I had made the wrong decision as neither of them would eat any branded baby food, which can often be a lot less hassle if you are out and about. Now, five years on, both eat a very healthy and varied diet – and will ask for fruit and veg as part of their meals and packed lunches. Don't get me wrong, they both have kiddie treats every day and love sweets and chocolate as much as any other child – but they also see pineapple, pomegranate, blueberries and suchlike as treats too! I would urge any parents to include as much varied fruit or veg as early as possible. It really does pay off and is well worth the effort.

Charles, dad to three sons

I live in France and my now-fifteen-year-old son was weaned the French way. I was told not to give rice, pasta or potatoes until after he was a year old as they are bland and just fill the baby up. Instead each week I had to introduce a new strong-tasting vegetable, e.g. aubergine, peppers, etc, and eventually adding fish or chicken. My son eats everything put in front of him and was even eating oysters at two years old. My elder two sons, now nineteen and seventeen, were much fussier as children, but now after eating at the schools here also eat everything. In France different food is never prepared for the children – they eat at the table with the adults and are given the same food. The system really works.

Hayley, mum to a ten-month-old daughter

My ten-month-old daughter Lauren and I had been invited to spend a day with my friend Catherine and her seven-month-old son William. On the menu, finger food for all, which included grapes cut into halves so the children wouldn't choke. As I stripped the kids off later for their bath, I screamed to Catherine: 'Lauren has slugs in her nappy!' Catherine came running through and scooped Lauren up whilst I cleaned the 'slugs' up in a panic. She then burst out laughing and explained to me that the slugs were in fact whole halves of grapes that clearly Lauren had swallowed without chewing! We still laugh about this to this day.

Chapter 10

Moving and Grooving

I can't tell you how much I wanted to be there to see Betsy do things for the first time. I'd have been gutted if I'd missed her do anything important. I say 'important' because some things, like the first time she let out a loud bottom burp in public (we were in Tesco – the shame), I could quite happily have missed! I know that if I'd have come home from work to my mum or Lee telling me that

Betsy had crawled, walked or said her first word I would have cried for hours, and no doubt felt guilty too. My mum told me my dad had been looking after me the day I decided to crawl for the first time and she had been really upset.

I can't imagine what it would be like to be a full-time working mum and have no choice but to go out each day to provide for the family. From what friends in that situation have told me, it can be really tough at times to return home to your little one and whoever has been doing the childcare to hear about the things they have been up to. It must feel like being torn in opposite directions between the need to earn a wage and have a successful career and also the natural desire to be at home with your little one to experience all their exciting developments first-hand. Us girls are masters at multitasking but even superwoman would struggle with that dilemma. The key is to strike a balance that works for you, something my friends refer to as 'the elusive juggle'. Miraculously, I was around as Betsy reached all her important milestones and I now have memories I will treasure forever and about a thousand photos and videos too!

There's a downside to these milestones though. Yes, they are a wonderful way of watching your child grow and develop, but you can fall into the trap of comparing your little one to others of the same age. It's very easy to get yourself in a tizz as a result. When Betsy was just over a year old I used to dread a certain activity we'd do at a local baby class we go to called Monkey Music, which involved the mums holding hands with their little ones and walking round in a circle. As every other toddler walked nicely next to their mums I was left carrying

Betsy, who was a big heavy lump at this point, because she was yet to master the art of putting one foot in front of the other. I may have been imagining it but it felt like all the other mums were staring at me.

My paranoia is not without reason: I've been to my fair share of mother-and-baby groups where the mums have done nothing but compare their perfect offspring to others and show off about how their little one is developing at a quicker pace than everyone else. It's ridiculous. I'm all for providing stimulation and interacting as much as possible to bring on development but I'm sure some mums are there with flash cards and foreign language books the moment they bring their babies home.

All babies develop different skills at different rates, especially in the early days. I've heard people say that babies are either walkers or talkers, and this does seem to be the case. I remember sitting there at one of the groups thinking, 'God, if the competition is this fierce when they're this age, what the hell is it going to be like when Betsy starts school?'

Me, I'm just happy for Betsy to do things in her own time, on one condition – that I'm there to see it!

Rolling, Rolling, Rolling...

Betsy was around the five-month mark when she rolled over for the first time. It was a real surprise, too – one minute she was doing her daily tummy time on her play mat, wriggling around and throwing some shapes with her friend Sophie the Giraffe, and the next she was on her back, arms and legs flailing around in the air! It wasn't just a lucky roll either; she'd obviously been working on it for quite a while, because she'd perfected the move and went on to do it again and again ... she was on a roll (sorry, I just had to).

Suddenly I had to pay much more attention to what was around and where I positioned her. Gone were the days when I could lay her on the bed or sit her on the sofa, pop cushions around her and know she'd be safe while I got up for a few seconds to grab the phone. Up until now I had been changing her on a changing table that was waist-height, but she was trying to roll about so much while I was changing her nappy that I had to move everything to the floor. Of course I've never left her unattended, but just the thought of her rolling off the mat from about three feet up scared the life out of me. I've heard that one of the most common accidents that children's A&E departments see are babies falling off changing mats. I'd also just heard a story about a friend's sister who didn't realise quite how mobile her little one was and put her in one of those Bumbo chairs on the kitchen table. As she turned round to grab something from the work surface, the baby wriggled out of the chair and fell straight on to the tiled floor. After a trip to the hospital, I'm pleased to say she suffered nothing more than a big bruise to the head and she went on to make a full recovery. She was extremely lucky.

Thankfully, so far Betsy has never suffered more than a grazed knee but there have been occasions when things could have been worse. There was one incident not long after Betsy had perfected her full roll when I lay her on the sofa and sat with her until she fell asleep. Once she was out for the count I put a row of cushions on the floor next to the sofa as I had always done and plonked myself in a chair facing her to read a magazine. I must have been exhausted after suffering a couple of sleepless nights and consequently dozed off. I woke up to find Betsy looking up at me from the cushions on the floor with a big smile as if to say, 'Look at me, I got down here all by myself!' I spent the next few days feeling awful and running through endless 'what ifs?' in my head.

A Visit from the Tooth Fairy

Of course milestones aren't just limited to changes in your baby's physical abilities – it's also fascinating to monitor the changes in their physical appearance too. The first tooth coming through is the big one, first because it heralds a new change in your baby's ability to bite and chew proper food, but also because it's often such a drama for the little one as the sharp little tooth starts cutting through their gums.

The first indication we had that Betsy had started teething was when she was four and a half months old and began dribbling constantly. And when I say dribbling I mean she was completely soaking everything she wore. Any clothes I put her in were wet within minutes. I had to start putting her in lighter-coloured tops and kept an endless supply of bibs to hand to save me from having to change her quite so often.

Along with the dribble came permanently rosy cheeks, a runny nose and runny nappies, as teething systematically affects a baby's whole system. I'd regularly check her temperature to make sure it wasn't high, and try to ease the discomfort by smothering her gums in teething gel, giving her some of those great teething granules or tempting her with soothers I'd cooled in the fridge. Anything to take her attention away from gumming any random item she could get her hands on. Everything she held in her hands went straight to her mouth, it didn't matter what it was – remote controls, mobile phones and even socks. You name it, it all ended up soaked in dribble.

After what must literally have been litres of dribble, Betsy finally cut her first tooth at six months, which was a momentous occasion and certainly worth all the fuss. When the teeth are just under the surface of the gums you can see them as little grey bumps trying to get out, but when they actually come through and you see the brilliant white enamel for the first time it makes you realise just how quickly your little one is growing up. The teeth further back in the mouth caused the most trouble and it would break my heart when Betsy would push her finger into her mouth and look at me as if to say, 'Mummy it's hurting, do something please.' But sometimes the only thing you can do for your child is give them lots of love and cuddles. Since she was born I've been strict about Betsy sleeping in her Moses basket or cot so we don't make a rod for our own back, but when she was teething I threw that rule out the window and would often bring her into our bed and give her plenty of comfort.

Of course once she had teeth and was learning how to use them we wanted to make sure they were kept clean and healthy so we introduced her brushing routine early and made a song and dance about it so it's loads of fun. I start off by cleaning them properly and then give her the brush so she can do it herself. She gets a real sense of achievement from it: she cleans away and then claps herself and stamps her feet afterwards!

While her last couple of teeth were coming through she suffered from a really bad cold, which added to her misery. She couldn't sleep at all when lying down, so I brought her into bed with me for a couple of nights and propped her up so she was comfortable and could get some rest. She snored constantly and I lay there wide-awake, half smiling and half desperate to get some sleep. As she finally got over her cold and got her energy back I was left totally exhausted, so my mum came and stayed while I spent a night in a hotel to catch up on sleep before a long day at work. It was the best night's sleep I'd had in a long time and I was so pleased and relieved to be in a quiet room that I announced my joy on Twitter. BIG MISTAKE! I received a flood of abusive replies about what a bad parent I was not being at home with Betsy. It was as if everyone thought I'd left Betsy on her own rather than in the very capable hands of her grandma. Once again I let it get to me – I'm still waiting for the thicker skin I've ordered to arrive.

Getting Mobile

With her new white tooth gleaming and her rolling skills well developed, Betsy turned her attention to the next challenge: crawling. Betsy is definitely a little explorer at heart and once she'd learned to roll over, she seemed more eager than ever to move around. Even though she wasn't able to do any more than a roll from her back to her front or vice versa she would look around with absolute intent and stretch her back and almost strain her neck as if she was willing herself to move to another point. You could tell that she couldn't wait to become more mobile so my mum and I decided to help her by showing her how it's done. The pair of us must have looked like we had lost the plot as we crawled around the living room on our hands and knees while Betsy sat watching us. We were having a moment where we had both realised how silly we must have looked and were in fits of giggles when Betsy decided to join in and actually managed a bit of a shuffle. It was so funny because as soon as she moved that little bit she looked me straight in the eye and burst out laughing as if to say, 'This is it – there's definitely no stopping me now!' Then with absolute determination she spent the rest of the day practising her shuffling to the point that by teatime she was actually mobile.

When I say shuffling that's exactly what it was: a bum shuffle. She would sit up and use her left leg to shuffle along while her right leg dragged behind her. To say it looked a bit weird would be an understatement. I was a bit worried about it at first so I was relieved when I spotted a little boy at Monkey Music who was shuffling in exactly the same way as Betsy. Apparently it's just a transition phase although some babies just don't crawl in the traditional sense of the word. I became friends with his mum in the end because we would make a beeline for each other every week to compare notes. It was quite cute as Betsy now had a partner in her comedy shuffle crime.

Cool Cruiser

When Betsy hit the eight-month mark she began to pull herself up and stand while holding on to the furniture, then after a few days she plucked up the courage to move along or 'cruise', as it's know in baby circles. This began a whole new phase of exploration as she realised there was an exciting new world above floor level. She spent hours wandering around clinging on to whichever piece of furniture was closest, squealing and chattering away with excitement. Our flat is quite open-plan and all on one level so it was the ideal setting for her to learn to stand alone without encountering any stairs. The downside was that when she did come across her first small flight of steps while we were out and about she didn't quite know what to do. To my horror she used the typical toddler strategy of just throwing herself at them and damn the consequences. Luckily mummy and daddy were there to catch her.

As she used to reach out and randomly grab whatever was closest we realised that we had to immediately rearrange all of our household furniture and possessions to make them baby safe, and more importantly re-programme ourselves so we wouldn't leave cups of tea or anything remotely dangerous within reach. We did however make a point of keeping photo frames (without sharp edges) in the same places because I wanted to teach her what she could and shouldn't touch. She picked up the concept of 'no' really quickly and if I told her something was mummy's she generally left it alone. Unfortunately my very expensive patent leather Mulberry handbag seemed to be an exception to this rule and could usually be found being dragged behind Betsy as she cruised her way around the flat.

A Walk in the Park

Out of all the milestones Betsy has reached so far, her first steps were the most important to me. The first smile and first words are of course amazing, but in my mind becoming fully mobile is such a major leap forward in a baby's development, so I really wanted to see her do it myself. My mum told me that I was an early walker, taking my first steps at around nine months, so I'd assumed Betsy would take hers around the same time.

As it turned out she took a lot longer to start walking, finally putting one foot in front of the other at fifteen months. There were a few people who seemed to take pleasure in telling me Betsy was quite slow to walk but to be honest, even though I was really looking forward to seeing it happen, I wasn't in any hurry. I'd been warned by my mummy friends that things step up a gear once they do become fully mobile.

It was while I was filming *Run for Your Wife* that Betsy looked like she could be ready to walk. As this was a three-week schedule with no days off, I began stressing out that I was going to miss her first steps. What if I was out when it happened? I'd have been gutted and never forgiven myself. My mum was staying with us to help out with Betsy and she could see I was worrying about it. If something needed picking up from the shop I would ask Lee to go and would drag my heels when it came to leaving the house in the morning. Anything to spend more time with Betsy. My mum sat me down and quite rightly pointed out that I could be in the next room making a cup of tea or having a pee when it happened so I needed to chill out. Those few words put it all into perspective for me and calmed me down a lot.

One afternoon while I was on set I saw my mum's number appear on my phone and I swear my heart skipped a beat. I felt tears welling up before I'd even answered. Of course there I was jumping the gun again; she was calling for something completely different. However, she told me that Betsy was so close to walking she thought it would be a day at most before she was a toddler. I rushed off set that evening and had a word with the production crew to see if it would be possible to take the next day off, but the best they could do was offer me a later call time, for which I was extremely grateful.

The very next morning I was sitting on the floor tidying Betsy's toys when out of the corner of my eye I spotted Betsy up on her feet having a little wobble as if she was adjusting her internal gyroscope. I just knew this was the moment she was going to walk. Her determination and concentration were palpable. I turned to her and with the biggest grin on my face I opened my arms. She set off and did four steps before falling into my lap. She was so pleased with herself and even gave herself a little clap. I was just thrilled to have seen it – call me bonkers but I'm sure she waited until I was around.

Needless to say I grabbed my camera and filmed her doing her next few wobbly steps so I could show Daddy when he got home from work. It was a good thing that I got photographic evidence, as it was almost two weeks before she walked again. I think when she sat down after her first wobbly walk she thought, 'Sod this, it's much harder work than it looks.' She'd also clearly worked out that if she sat in one spot and pointed then she would get whatever she wanted anyway.

Despite her reluctance to show off her new skill I was so proud that I told anyone who would listen. Whenever we had visitors I would put Betsy in the middle of the room in the hope she'd dazzle us with a hop, skip and jump. Unfortunately, unlike her mum, she suffered from stage fright and just wouldn't do it on demand. I soon worked out that if I pretended not to look at her she'd then get up and walk around without a care in the world. Betsy became a fully fledged walker at sixteen months and crawling became so last season.

Little Miss Chatterbox

There's quite often a feeling of competition between parents over whose name gets spoken first but I read that 99 per cent of the time a baby will say 'Dada' first as it's easier for them. I was absolutely delighted to hear Betsy say Dada for the first time at eleven months, I went round the flat pointing at every photo of Lee and repeating it over and over again. I tried her with 'Mummy' and 'Nanny' as we pointed at the other photos but she was having none of it. Naturally Lee was absolutely delighted to hear her say Dada for the first time, and he had a good few days of pride of place in Betsy's vocabulary until she decided to start saying Momma too. At that point it was as if she forgot how to say Dada, because it didn't get another look-in for a couple of weeks, much to Lee's disappointment. He would kneel in front of Betsy and carefully mouth 'D-A-D-A' but she still wouldn't repeat it.

We've paid a lot of attention to Betsy's speech and understanding of words, and it's something that I'm really passionate about. I know someone who is as quiet as a mouse and even when surrounded by good friends rarely joins in the conversation, so when her baby came along she hardly spoke to her. Perhaps as a result, her little one was really late to talk. Whenever I show Betsy pictures in books or point to animals while out on our walks I always make sure I use the correct name so she doesn't get confused. It must be tricky trying to learn a new language when you're being taught a dog is also a doggie, a woof-woof or whatever other nicknames there are.

I also love reading to Betsy and I make sure she gets a bedtime story every evening. That was something I missed out on when I was growing up because my mum went back to work when I was one and didn't have the luxury of time to read to three kids. As a result I was never really into books, although I've made up for that these days in the sheer volume of gossip mags I get through instead.

Apart from Betsy's first word, the other talking milestones I was privileged to witness were her first proper phrases: 'bye bye', 'yes please' and 'love you Mummy', which just melted my heart. Of all the new words and phrases I don't think anything will pull on your heartstrings like the first time your little one tells you they love you. Betsy was sixteen months when she came into the bathroom one morning and just said it out of the blue. I almost fell over. It was as clear as anything. It's obviously something she's picked up from when we tell her we love her. Sadly no matter how many times Lee tried to teach her 'I love you Daddy' she wouldn't say it for ages, much to his heartbreak.

The first morning she said 'bye bye' to me was perfectly in context as I walked out of the front door, and it was so natural that I didn't even notice at first. It was only when I was on the pavement outside that it sank in so I ran back in to give her a big kiss and a hug. Her 'yes please' is actually more of a 'yes peas' but I'm just so happy she's picking up polite mannerisms that it fills me with pride every time she says it.

Moving on and Growing up

Despite the criticism, sleepless nights and the stressing over the possibility of missing them, each milestone has been wonderful and a little reminder of just how quickly my baby girl is growing up. I'll often watch Betsy happily entertaining herself with her toys and wonder where the time has gone. It seems like one day she was this tiny helpless baby in my arms, and the next she's a little person toddling around and doing her best to boss me about. It's such an old adage and one you would expect your granny or granddad to come out with, so I'll put on my best croaky voice as I say, 'They grow up so fast!'

A word from my Twitter followers

Angie, mum to a two-year-old son

My son Joshua cut his first tooth at around six months old. The teething started with red cheeks, lots of dribble, a few tears and a number of sleep-deprived nights for us both! I found teething granules a great help and I also invested in an amber teething necklace, which worked too. Joshua wears it through the day and I take it off just before bedtime. He's now two years old and has nineteen teeth and has just one tooth to go – happy days!

Helen, mum to a six-month-old daughter

I was fortunate that I was with my children for most of their milestones. The only thing I wasn't the first to see was when my daughter properly laughed. She had smiled and had a little giggle lots of times but it was while a friend was looking after her that she laughed uncontrollably while they were playing a game. It was lovely to see her enjoy herself so much but part of me felt quite upset that it wasn't me that had made her laugh like that first.

Matt, dad to a one-year-old son

One day I finished work a couple of hours early and when I got home I hid around the corner to the kitchen in the dining room and began saying, 'Elijah, Elijah!' I heard him instantly stop what he was doing and crawl as quickly as he could into the dining room. He couldn't quite see me so he called 'Daaaaaaaaaaddddda!' at which point I came into view. He had the biggest smile on his face. I nearly cried as it was the first time he had said my name.

Karen, mum to a six-year-old son

When my second son was born with Down's Syndrome I had to let go of all the worries about whether he was going to hit milestones on time, because he obviously wasn't. He took his first steps just in time for his second birthday. I learned to slow down and appreciate him reaching his milestones in his own time and in his own sweet way. I also learned not to get so dispirited if any of my other children reached them late. It doesn't really matter when a child reaches a milestone, what matters is that they get there in the end.

Sharon, mum to a four-year-old son

I never wanted children. I knew I didn't possess the gene, the inclination, the desire or patience to raise a child. I became accidentally pregnant at the age of thirty-eight. Fantastic pregnancy, horrendous birth. I had a fourth-degree tear and had to have immediate surgery. I simply didn't bond with my son and felt complete indifference to him. I had spent so much time hearing about this mythical 'thunderbolt' of instant love that you're meant to feel for your child, but for me it wasn't there. My son was fed, clothed, cuddled, kissed and wanted for nothing, but whilst I could say I loved him I certainly didn't feel it. There was no doubt I had PND but for very valid reasons I didn't pursue a diagnosis or treatment. One day when he was four it happened. Out of nowhere. He had been trying to reach the light pull in the toilet for ages and this day he managed it. He was elated and ran to me filled with joy. I swung him round and WHAM! It hit me, square in the heart. I loved him, I made him, he was mine, I would die for him and above everything else, I felt it with every fibre of my being till I thought I would explode with love. And boy, did I cry! He looked at me in such a grown-up way with an expression that said, 'I knew you'd feel it one day.' That was a major milestone for me.

Caroline, mum to a two-year-old son

When my boy was nearly nine months old he hadn't started crawling but was getting on to all fours and then falling back down. I had gone to pick him up from my mum after work and he wanted something on the other side of the room. I said to him, 'You can have it if you crawl over to it,' and he got into the crawling position and then moved forward two spaces for the first time ever. It's one of the many magic moments that I am so happy I was able to witness.

Michaela, mum to a two-year-old son

My son was born ten weeks' premature, weighing 2 lb 4 oz. A big milestone for us was getting him home after eight weeks in special care.

Emma, mum to a one-year-old daughter

My baby girl is one and seriously smart! Her dad is half-Chinese and his culture is very important to him, so since she could talk and understand words we've been teaching her the Chinese and English words for everything. She knows 'nose', 'hair', 'ears', 'lights' and 'water' and has even taken to asking for her milk in Chinese too! When she goes near things she shouldn't she turns to tell me 'no' before I can say it to her! We're very proud of her.

Chapter 11

A First Time for Everything

The first few months or even years of motherhood can seem like a blur when you look back so it's important to take as many pictures as possible to remind you. Taking care of the day-to-day mummy duties can often leave little time for anything else, and you'll find those early days of snapping away merrily like David Bailey while your baby lies in one place are replaced by a new era of constant tidying up and cleaning everything in sight with baby wipes once your little one becomes mobile. So when it came to important 'firsts' I wanted to remember forever, like Betsy's first Christmas, birthday and holiday, I made sure friends and family took plenty of pictures to make up for my lack of snapping.

Of course, not all firsts are worth recording for posterity. The first time Betsy was due an injection, at three months old, I was absolutely dreading taking her. My mate Karen had said she hated taking Rose for her jabs as she screamed the place down. When I took her to the clinic Betsy looked so small and I hated the thought of anything hurting her but of course I knew she needed to have them. When the nurse gave her the injection she flinched a little bit so I waved a toy in front of her to distract her and she was fine, much to my relief. I'm sure it's the parents who suffer the most. They did get worse as she got older and I'm dreading the injections when she is three!

First Holiday

Betsy was seven months old when she received her first stamp in her passport. I was desperate for a break but unfortunately Lee was busy working so, with his blessing, I got the girls together – my mum, best mate Tamara and of course Betsy – and we all headed off to the sun for a week.

Although Lee wasn't coming with us he was certainly involved in the planning because I had trouble deciding where to go. There seemed so much to consider now a little one was involved, from flight times to facilities to weather conditions. The list seemed endless. In the end we decided on Dubai. It's not really the kind of place I had expected us to travel to, but it had everything going for it – the weather was forecast as warm but not too hot (it was December), the flight times and duration coincided perfectly so we could catch a late departure and Betsy could sleep through, and there was loads to do indoors as well as outside so we could keep Betsy out of the sun without any of us getting bored.

I've always been one for taking a lot of stuff on holiday but packing for the first trip with Betsy was just crazy. I had all of our clothes in separate piles on the bed and Betsy's pile was easily as big as mine. Not only was I packing her a couple of outfits per day to accommodate the heat and cool air conditioning but there were also the essentials such as nappies and milk to contend with. I wanted to make sure I had enough to last the trip, as I didn't want to waste time shopping or having to experiment with brands I'm not familiar with. As I remembered something else that was essential for Betsy I'd have to take out another dress or pair of shoes from my bag. All in all it must have taken me a full weekend to pack.

I was rather nervous about the flight as I wasn't sure how Betsy would react but at least I had my mum and Tamara to help me keep her entertained and carry all the hand luggage. I'd booked a night flight in the hope that she would sleep through, but what if she cried the whole time? I remember one particular flight to LA when I was sat a row behind a couple with a tiny baby. I watched as people looked over as they boarded the plane as if to say, 'Oh no, I hope I'm not sitting too close.' The poor parents were in such a state as the baby cried for four hours straight. I heard people tutting and caught someone throwing a dirty look from across the aisle. There was nothing the unfortunate parents could do. Luckily I managed to keep Betsy occupied for the first couple of hours before the lights were dimmed. She then promptly downed a bottle of milk and was out for the count for the rest of the flight.

When we got there the first thing that hit us was the heat, even in the early hours of the morning. It turned out that Dubai was experiencing a heatwave for the time of year so our choice to go somewhere with indoor facilities definitely proved to be the right one. We'd booked to stay in a massive hotel, which is part of a larger leisure complex that has shopping malls, restaurants and even a massive aquarium built in. I knew between Mum and I we would be able to take it in turns to look after Betsy and keep her out of the sun, and there'd still be plenty of time to top up our tans.

I would take Betsy out for walks early in the morning before breakfast so it was still nice and cool, and we'd have a little play together. She loved sitting on the beach and we had the best time building sandcastles, although she seemed determined to fit as much sand in her mouth as possible – maybe we should have had breakfast first!

This holiday was also the first time Betsy had been near the sea so I'd been really looking forward to taking her for a dip. I'd bought her one of those floating rings with a seat in so her legs could dangle through and she could have a good old kick around in the water. We all headed down to the beach late afternoon when the sun had cooled down but the water was still warm. As we approached the sea Betsy looked at me for reassurance and I gave her a big smile and told her we were going for a splish splash – something I'd always say when we were going swimming in the local pool back at home. I gently lowered her into the water and straight away she began kicking her legs. She gradually got braver and after five minutes she was laughing as she turned herself round in circles and bobbed up and down on the waves. We made it a daily ritual, at least until the second-to-last day when I spotted a jellyfish in our usual spot, putting an abrupt end to our fun in the sea. Thank God Betsy didn't get stung – or any of us for that matter!

We did have a couple of cooler days so I hired one of those giant sunbeds you see next to pools at posh hotels nowadays. It looked more like a four-poster bed and had awnings over the top so we were totally shielded from the sun. I covered Betsy from head to toe in factor-fifty suncream and bought her a little sun hat. She looked really grown-up in her swimming costume and hat, lying flat out sparko in the middle of the bed while my mum, Tamara and I all tried to squeeze in round the edges and look comfortable.

I know there are loads of opinions on internet forums on whether you should adjust your baby to a different time zone while you're away or not. Dubai is four hours ahead of the UK but I decided not to worry too much. If you have ever suffered from jet lag you will know how painful it is to try and keep awake when all you want to do is curl up and sleep. So I allowed Betsy to sleep when she was tired and on the odd occasion when she woke up during the night I played with her for an hour before popping her back in her cot. It worked a treat.

All in all it was a real shame Lee wasn't with us but my first holiday with Betsy was amazing. However, I also learned that as fun as holidays are with a little one, they're generally not very relaxing – and they're not going to be for the foreseeable future. It actually made a really nice change to be on the go as most of the holidays I've been on in the past have involved lying on a sun lounger by the pool and reading magazines for the whole duration. Those days are clearly over!

First Christmas

Coming back from Dubai we were immediately launched into the Christmas season. I'm a big fan of this time of year so it doesn't take much for me to get into the seasonal spirit. But with seven-month-old Betsy in the flat to join in the festive fun my Christmas cheer went through the roof! All of the decorations were up bang on the first day of December and I'd bought a fibre-optic tree that didn't have any baubles so there was nothing she could break or put in her mouth. Of course it was a given that we'd dress Betsy up but it was a tough choice as there were so many super-cute costumes in the shops. I narrowed it down so in the end it was a toss-up between a mini reindeer and Mrs Claus. I let Lee make the final decision; he doesn't get many of those so he was delighted. She was to be Mrs Claus. Betsy rocked the look!

It's tough deciding what to do for Christmas even before you throw a new baby into the mix. Everyone wanted to see Betsy so we thought long and hard about how we could get to see everyone and make it fair. I would have loved to have catered for both sets of grandparents and our siblings round at ours for Christmas Day but it would have been a bit much. In the end we spent Christmas Day at Lee's parents as they don't get to see us as often as my parents and Betsy is their first grandchild. We then headed to my parents on Boxing Day and had a 'second' Christmas there, as many families end up doing.

Despite Betsy having absolutely no idea what was going on, or even what a present was, we still bought her toys and wrapped them up for her to open. I did all the wrapping and of course didn't take into account her delicate little fingers, so not only could she not open them, I found it difficult enough myself. It was only after Christmas that a friend told me she always uses tissue paper to wrap her little one's pressies, which I think is a genius idea. In the end we had a great Christmas and everyone was happy, especially Betsy who was spoilt rotten.

I have mates whose parents pile on the pressure when it comes to making plans for Christmas Day and it ends up turning into a nightmare – they dread Christmas and very nearly have a breakdown. I feel really lucky that there's no stress from either set of grandparents, and I hope one day I'll be the same with Betsy when she's grown up.

Betsy absolutely loved her second Christmas, because at nineteen months she had a much better understanding that something special was going on. I never feel Christmas lasts long enough so I put the decorations up in the middle of November. Betsy thought this was a great idea and was giggling away as she helped me. We even put fairy lights over Betsy's cot and read loads of Christmas books to teach her about Santa, Rudolf and snowmen. We did the reverse of the previous year and spent Christmas Day with my family and Boxing Day with Lee's. Betsy looked gorgeous in her pretty party dresses and was hyper for two days straight. She was spoilt rotten once again, her favourite present being a Peppa Pig campervan which is a big tent where she sits and plays with her toys. She wolfed down two Christmas dinners, sprouts and all – we'll see how long that lasts for.

First Birthday

I'm not too sure where Betsy's first year went! It seemed like one moment I was bringing our bundle of joy home for the first time and the next Lee and I were discussing how to celebrate her first birthday.

It's really easy to get carried away with birthday ideas – especially for the all-important inaugural one – and in the past few years we've witnessed footballers and actors spending up to £100,000 on first birthday parties. Back in the real world, Lee and I decided we'd like to keep Betsy's celebrations to a small close-family-and-friends affair. It was also important for us to make sure our families had a nice day too. When my grandparents were alive they celebrated most of our early birthdays with us and loved to spoil us so I wanted our parents to have the same opportunity with their granddaughter.

The one thing I did decide to splash out on was Betsy's outfit. I don't believe in spending lots of money on baby clothes as a rule because they tend to get covered in food and dribble and they grow out of them so fast. But this was a special occasion, and I knew her first birthday outfit would be something I'd like to keep for when she's older – another item for the memory box! Of course, as with most things us mums buy for our babies, it was more for me rather than Betsy but she looked absolutely gorgeous in the little dress and cardigan by the designer Rachel Riley. It was worth every penny of the sixty-five pounds I paid for it and it has been duly cleaned and put out of the way so it doesn't get passed on by mistake.

All things considered, we decided on a little tea party in our garden. Fortunately the weather was perfect – perhaps due to my last-minute sun dance. As well as our families we invited some of my friends who have kids, a few of whom are Betsy's age. To keep the little ones (and some big ones) entertained, we booked the girl who runs the local Monkey Music class to come along so we could all have a sing-along. On the big day there we all were, sitting in a circle clapping, singing and blowing bubbles. As the last guest left I was exhausted whereas Betsy was still racing around. Thank God it's only once a year!

First Day at Nursery

When Betsy was eighteen months old there came a point when if she could talk (I'd have been seriously boasting – joke!) she would have probably said, 'Mum, it's time for me to make new friends.' I also felt she would benefit from a bit more interaction with others her age on a regular basis, as she would light up if another toddler paid her any attention at the park.

She'd also been having so much fun at the mother-and-baby groups I'd been taking her to. We'd been regulars at Monkey Music since Betsy was five months old. You sit in a circle, sing and play maracas (well, the mums do while the babies watch in wonderment). It's really stimulating for the babies and the mums get to have a good chat afterwards. Rachel Stevens takes her daughter Amelie too, so we catch up each week on what our little ones have been up to. We never talk about work stuff – it's all 'Betsy this' and 'Amelie that'. We still go every week now and Betsy gets seriously excited whenever the date rolls around. She's gone from one of the youngest in the group to being a mini grown-up with plenty of confidence – she also has great rhythm, which I'm convinced is partly due to these classes.

It was definitely time to find a nursery for Betsy to attend regularly for a few mornings a week. I have to admit I was slightly apprehensive at first, as she had been receiving one-on-one attention since she was born. On the flipside, I knew that if she didn't spend more time with other children she might find it difficult to cope when she goes to school and is surrounded by loads of other kids. I also didn't want Betsy to get bored of being in the same places and of playing with the same toys, so a change of scenery was definitely in order. The hunt began!

I must admit I hadn't realised just how difficult finding a suitable nursery would be. Naturally I wanted to find one that had a good reputation and was nearby (preferably within walking distance), but that was easier said than done. When I found a nursery that came highly recommended it had a ridiculous waiting list, and I discovered that many nurseries wouldn't take little ones under two, as they are not set up for babies. Eventually I found a great playgroup which was just around the corner and enrolled Betsy straight away.

Of course there I was, first day, not wanting to leave her. To make matters worse, Betsy didn't want to let me go either, clinging to me as if her life depended on it. One of the girls suggested I just leave immediately if I felt comfortable because she'd be fine once I'd gone, but I didn't have it in me. In the end I went for the good old distraction technique – I led her to a doll in a pram and as soon as she started playing with it I made a dash for it. At least that way I didn't have to walk out as Betsy sobbed, 'Mummeeee!'

The playgroup leader told me the tears were short-lived and Betsy loves it there now. She's come on leaps and bounds in the last few months she's been attending. I see her playing so nicely with the other little ones when I sneak in to collect her – I'll watch her for a couple of minutes as she cooks a cake in the toy kitchen with her friend and my heart will melt when they sit down together to pretend to eat it. Nursery has really helped her to learn to share toys with the other children. And she loves to get stuck into the messy play, which is great for me too – I'd much rather her clothes get covered in paint while she's at nursery than my cream carpet getting ruined at home!

For me there's only one major downside to putting your child in nursery, and that's how much it costs. Hands up if like me you've almost fallen over backwards in shock at the price of childcare! Don't get me wrong, I know Lee and I are very lucky to have steady well-paid work but I just can't believe how much it's ended up costing. When I was given the documentation at the first nursery I went to take a look around, I honestly thought they had accidentally put 'per day' when they really meant 'per week'! It's ridiculous. Sometimes it feels like you're working just to cover childcare.

That said, knowing that Betsy is in safe hands while I'm at work is a huge weight off my mind. She also seems to have grown up a little every time I collect her and seeing her mix with lots of other children and have so much fun makes up for the expense – well, almost! Once again, it's a sign that my little girl is growing up fast.

A word from my Twitter followers

Lesley, mum to eighteen-month-old twin sons

It took us eighteen months to pluck up the courage to take our twin boys on holiday. We had been well warned to forget the 'lazing by the pool recovering from hangover'-type holidays of the past, so felt we were well-prepared. We boarded the plane and within a few minutes realised one of the boys had a tummy upset. After a pretty unpleasant flight, made slightly better by the fact that the passengers around us were too drunk to notice the awful stench, we made our way to the hotel. Next day I took the well twin to the welcome meeting whilst his dad looked after sick boy. The meeting was then cut short as my 'well' son started running around the room with diarrhoea escaping from his nappy. I grabbed him and ran from the room, weeping, and spent the first week of the holiday in our room – which must have stank to high heaven – trying to keep the boys hydrated. All this while also trying to communicate with a Portuguese doctor, and attempting to translate the small print on the medicine he prescribed. In the end I resorted to letting them drink flat coke, which of course they loved! The bug passed and all was well until the day of departure when one of my sons went missing by the pool. One minute there, the next gone. We panicked quite a lot and swore we'd never go on holiday ever again. Eventually I found him in the toddler pool sitting up to his waist, fully clothed, fifteen minutes before the bus was due to leave to take us to the airport!

Sarah, mum to a three-year-old daughter

For my daughter's first Christmas I started shopping in September, manically piling the pram high with bags, risking near exhaustion in order to create the 'perfect' day – no pressure! The grandparents fought over who would host their granddaughter's first Christmas and the in-laws won. My daughter loved the lights and glittery paper – which she tried to eat – then was bored after opening one present and just enjoyed rolling around on the floor. We had to do it all again with my parents on Boxing Day!

Lessons learned: six-month-olds aren't fussed about Christmas, so don't waste money on piles of pressies. Time their nap so you can actually eat your dinner while it's hot! And don't risk your health worrying about buying elaborate gifts for friends and family – you and baby should take priority.

Ruth, mum of two daughters

My second daughter was born a month before Christmas, some years ago now. She was born at home, which was a magical experience, and she was such a good baby, sleeping through the night every night for the first month … until Christmas Eve, that is! She woke at 1 am (what?!) wanting a quick feed, nappy change and cuddle, then went back to sleep. But she then woke again at 4 am (unheard of). This time her big sister (then aged two and a half) also woke up, and solemnly informed us that baby had woken because she wanted to see what Father Christmas looked like, and what he was going to leave in her stocking.

Maxine, mum of two daughters

Last year me and my husband had our first Christmas with our beautiful adopted daughters, ages five and three, who came to live with us in the summer. My husband and I have been together for twenty years and have always wanted children and have been through IVF and a tough adoption process to eventually become a family.

On Christmas Eve the girls and I made mince pies together and then sorted the presents under the Christmas tree into piles for our family. The house was warm and Christmassy and my husband had gone out to get last-minute bits so it was just us three. As the girls set about organising the presents I stopped and watched them, all full of excitement, busily working together and taking their task of sorting presents very seriously. Suddenly John Lennon's voice came over the radio singing, 'So this is Christmas...' They both went quiet and my little three-year-old stopped and looked up towards the music. She got up on to her feet and started dancing. She looked so full of joy and so beautiful in her pretty red dress and with her ringletty hair bouncing up and down. I felt so overcome that I burst into tears. She stopped and came over to hug me. I told her, 'I'm crying because you both make me so happy.' She smiled and put her little arms around my neck and gave me a kiss. Then we all danced together and held hands. All three of us have had our struggles and Christmas was the most magical wish come true. I felt truly blessed and have done every day since I became their mum.

Helen, mum to three sons

We went to Lindisfarne in Northumbria to celebrate my oldest son's first birthday. He is named Aidan after Saint Aidan of Lindisfarne. We took a birthday cake to the beach at dusk and had a bit of trouble keeping the candle lit in the sea breeze. The cake was in the shape of a dog's face and it had a large black solid icing nose. Aidan loved the singing and the candle but what he wanted most was to eat the dog's nose. We let him eat the whole thing and the nappy consequences the next day were quite spectacular, I can tell you!

Lorna, mum to a fourteen-month-old daughter

My daughter's first birthday was a big affair – on the actual day we had a little party at home and then at the weekend we hired a hall and had a big party for fifty people with games and lots of party food.

Samantha, mum to a five-year-old son

We were really worried about Zach's first day at nursery as he'd never been in the care of anyone else other than family before. When we dropped him off he disappeared off straight away so we left him to it, and by the time I came to pick him up three hours later he looked very tired from all his activity. We took him home for his lunch and he vanished upstairs to play. After a while we thought it had gone quiet so went to check on him. I went into his room and he wasn't there, checked the bathroom – not there either – then, starting to panic, I rushed into our room but there was no sign of him. I was stood on the landing on the verge of tears when my husband went back into our room and called me in. There he was, lying underneath a pillow with a foot peeking out. As I burst into tears of relief Zach woke up, looked at me and said, 'Mum, why are you sad?' I told him I couldn't find him and was worried, and he replied, 'I'm OK, Mum, I'm a big boy now. I was tired from playing with trains and I wanted to dream about nursery!' I never have any worries about him going to school now. He loves going every day and at least now he's too big to hide under a pillow!

Kirsten, mum to a nine-year-old daughter

My little girl Gemma started nursery aged six months. Daddy dropped her off, as I just couldn't cope with it. I really didn't want to have to say cheerio to her. Needless to say she had a brilliant time there, and it turned out that going to nursery wasn't her only first that day: by the time she got home from nursery she had cut her first two teeth!

Ruth, mum to a three-year-old son

When I took my son to nursery the first time he was very shy and clearly didn't want to be there at all. As I was talking to his teacher he told me he wanted to go to the toilet, so I took him and waited outside the door. I was waiting and waiting and eventually went in the bathroom to see that he had managed to lock the cubicle door from the inside. It seemed he didn't want to come out. As well as being shy my son can also be stubborn. The teacher went away to search for a ladder to use to climb over the toilet door and in the meantime I started begging for him to come out. Finally he opened the door. He has stayed a bit shy and not too happy for his first two years at nursery.

Claire, mum to a three-year-old daughter

I had to arrange a crèche for my first daughter, Rebecca, when I was still pregnant as the waiting lists in my area were quite long. I visited five places, asking various questions about staff turnover, food, discipline and so on, and making sure the places didn't smell of pee. When I visited the last one I went into one of the rooms to find eight toddlers sitting round a table in complete silence. I thought, this is a bit weird. Then one of the girls came in carrying toast, and they all cheered! That's when I knew this crèche was for us.

Chapter 12

Terrible Twos and Beyond

Before I climbed Mount Kilimanjaro, someone said to me that anyone who hasn't climbed it will never understand what it's like. It's almost as if there's an informal Kilimanjaro Appreciation Society. It's the same with parenting. Before you have kids you know all the soundbites and theories but until you go through it you won't truly understand. Becoming a parent not only changes your life but dominates pretty much all of your waking thoughts.

My first year and a half as a mum certainly changed everything for me. I went from stressing over what to wear on a TV show or to an event to worrying about whether I had enough nappies and wipes to see me through to my next big shop. My girly nights out were ditched in favour of cosy nights in with Lee, happy in the knowledge that our little girl was snuggled up and sound asleep in the next room. Whereas I used to be a workaholic, I'd now check Betsy's diary alongside my own to see if there were any baby groups or birthday parties that took precedence before I committed to anything.

The way we live at home has changed too. Before Betsy came along we'd spend most of our time in the kitchen/dining area of the flat and when my girlfriends came over we'd all sit round the breakfast bar having a natter. Nowadays, the kitchen is used just for cooking (and the odd party) and it's the living room – which is generally covered in Betsy's toys – that is the real hub of our home.

To be honest, during my pregnancy I had been dreading the flat becoming babyfied with toys, high chairs and buggies. Before meeting Lee I had lived there on my own for seven years and it had taken me long enough to get used to having his stuff around the place – although thankfully he's tidy so there are no pants, toenail clippings or body hair left lying around!

The reality is – and I'm as surprised by this as anyone who knows me – I find having Betsy's things strewn around the place extremely comforting. In fact I've grown to enjoy the tidying-up process of putting away all of Betsy's toys, washing up her bottles and wiping down the tables and chairs once she's in bed. Before becoming a mum there was nothing I loved more than a tidy peaceful home, but now give me the noise and chaos that comes with having a child any day of the week. There have been occasions when Lee has taken Betsy to visit her grandparents and I've stayed at home to catch up on work and to be honest I've felt lost and couldn't wait for them to get back. How things have changed!

Miss Independent

Betsy has grown up so quickly over the last year and a half and I have loved every minute of it – well, with the exception of when she decided to smash my favourite glass ring by repeatedly banging it on the tiled floor and the time she threw my phone in the bath. When I look back now, it all seems a bit of a blur so I'm glad I took plenty of photos and videos to remind me. As well as looking back on the fantastic times we've had so far, I've also spent a fair amount of time wondering what lies ahead in this exciting yet unpredictable journey.

Of course I have the terrible twos to contend with in the immediate future. I'm sure I've already had a taste of what's to come as Betsy began to test the boundaries and became extremely vocal when she hit sixteen months. She transformed into a little fashionista overnight, letting me know exactly what she wanted to wear each morning, and if I tried to dress her in something other than the outfit she had chosen she would throw a tantrum. Every morning without fail she would want her Minnie Mouse trainers on and she'd point into her wardrobe repeatedly saying, 'Minnie, Minnie, Minnie!' until they were securely on her feet. I bought the trainers for three pounds from a charity shop – they were almost new, so a great find. You can get some real bargains if you look in the right places and it goes to show that although it might sometimes feel like parents need bottomless purses, you can be thrifty and your little one won't mind at all. So while Betsy's Minnie trainers are rapidly wearing out, there are shoes and little boots that either I have bought or have been kindly passed on to us that Betsy is quickly growing out of without her putting a single toe in them! Including a lovely pair for the winter that cost me sixty pounds, I might add.

Betsy has also developed a rebellious streak. Previously if she'd got hold of something that we didn't want her to have we'd tell her it was 'Mummy's' or 'Daddy's' and she'd hand it back to us with a smile on her face. Now if we ask her for something she dashes off with it in the opposite direction and usually heads for her little hiding place behind the sofa. Just the other day I spent over an hour searching for the TV remote control so I could chill out and watch an episode of *Downton Abbey* I'd recorded. I eventually found it – you guessed it – behind the sofa. It'll definitely be the first place I look from now on.

I found it hard at first not to laugh when my little monkey was being mischievous. It's the cute smile she gives when she's up to no good that gets me. We own a house in Kent which we bought with a view to eventually moving there full time when Betsy goes to school, so for now we split our time pretty much evenly between north London and the countryside. I'd been teaching Betsy that the utility room at the house in Kent is out of bounds because I was worried she might get her hands on something harmful. She seemed to have got the message, then one afternoon when I had prepared her dinner and began opening the door to the utility room to fetch a clean bib she shouted, 'No, Mummy!' I turned to see a stern face and a little finger wagging at me. She had me in stitches. I'm just waiting for her to do it with the other hand on her hip and then the transformation to mini-me will be complete.

Is it just me or do all mums find the whole business of teaching their little one right from wrong a minefield? There are so many differing opinions depending on which book you read or which person you speak to. My friend Joely is a teaching assistant and has an extremely well-mannered eight-year-old daughter so I asked her for some advice on how to tackle Betsy's emerging 'cheeky' personality. She reassured me that her daughter Téa developed a naughty streak around sixteen months too, and that the only advice she would offer was to be consistent with both discipline when Betsy is being naughty and praise when she's being good.

She also suggested I introduce a naughty step, or naughty chair in our case as we don't have any steps in the flat. Joely said it worked wonders for her and I'd also seen it on the TV show *Supernanny*, so I decided to give it a go. The first time I tried to implement it was when Betsy had thrown her plate and cutlery on the floor once she had decided she was full. I took her out of the highchair, sat her on the naughty chair and she laughed at me before saying 'Watch TV?' Thankfully after a few more attempts she realised I meant business and it's now working a treat.

I have to hold my hands up to letting Betsy get away with being a madam on the odd occasion when we are out and about as sometimes I'd rather not cause a scene in public – kicking and screaming is never a good look. I do tell her she'll be sitting on the naughty chair when we get home though and always follow it through.

I feel it's really important to set the ground rules and stick to them because if I change my mind every five minutes about what is acceptable and what isn't, it will only confuse Betsy. Joely told me another story of how she fell out with a friend who refused to discipline her own daughter if she hadn't witnessed her misbehaving. As a result her child learned she could get away with anything when her mum was not around and only needed to behave when she was. One day the little one in question lashed out at Téa while she was at Joely's on a play date. When the mum returned she wouldn't believe her daughter had done anything wrong and insinuated that Téa must have provoked her. What a crazy situation – I'd like to think that if someone told me that Betsy had misbehaved behind my back I'd do everything I could to stop it happening again. It's not just because I don't want to be on the receiving end of a dressing-down from an irate parent at the school gate, but also because I'd like Betsy to grow up into a lovely, polite young lady.

School Daze

Before I entered into the world of motherhood I really had no idea how difficult and important choosing the right school would be, but once I followed a friend's advice and began looking into it I soon became obsessed with league tables and reputations. I did so much homework that I could literally name every school within a ten-mile radius from our flat in Hampstead and our place in Kent and give a rundown of their Ofsted report. It made looking for the right nursery seem like a walk in the park.

I have such fond memories of my school days and for me it's really important that Betsy enjoys school too. I attended the Sylvia Young Theatre School in West London from the ages of eleven to sixteen. There I was encouraged to be creative and confident through drama, alongside the regular curriculum of course. I would really love Betsy to do theatrical studies so she develops confidence in herself but I certainly won't be pushing her into following in her mum and dad's footsteps and treading the boards. Of course if she chooses to exercise her jazz hands I will help her every step of the way. Lee, on the other hand, is keen for her to get a 'proper' job – he'd be over the moon if she becomes a lawyer, doctor or accountant.

After days of researching the local schools in both areas I finally found a lovely little school in Kent. I took a look around the place and the children were really polite, plus the headmaster has two young boys of his own who both attend the school, which is a good sign. They have a theatre group where the little ones learn to play instruments, dance and perform. It also has a great Ofsted report for its tutoring, and because it's in the country there are amazing views over the rolling fields and loads of outdoors space to play in and explore. That's one great thing about going to school outside of a city – although I really enjoyed my schooling it was in an enclosed area (a renovated church to be exact) and the only outside space was tiny and covered in concrete. I'd have given anything to have had the same opportunities but in a nicer setting. Anyway, Betsy's now all enrolled and will start pre-school from the age of three and stay there, all being well, until she's sixteen.

It'll mean moving to Kent permanently which we don't mind at all. One good thing about the work Lee and I do is that we very rarely get caught in rush-hour traffic because of the odd hours we have to work, so basing ourselves in Kent and travelling back into London for stage shows or filming should be relatively easy. In fact it will probably be just as quick door-to-door as travelling from north to central London. Either way it's certainly a price we don't mind paying to make sure Betsy gets the best start possible.

Even the daily school run should be a pleasant journey because it's all down country lanes, so the only traffic I'm likely to encounter is the odd tractor. I'm really looking forward to getting to know the other mums at the school gate too and inviting Betsy's friends over for play dates. Being one of three siblings I was never allowed to invite my school friends over because there was barely enough room for my brother, sister and I to play, let alone anyone else! I plan to make up for it when it's Betsy's turn to have friends over by spoiling them rotten. Jelly and ice cream, anyone?

We may have settled on a school but I've got no idea how I'm going to react when the time finally arrives for me to drop my baby off for her first day. I know I'll be super-proud and happy for her to embark on a new journey but if my performance when Betsy started nursery is anything to go by I'll be in the playground with tears running down my face, telling her we can go home if she can't face it. Meanwhile Lee will be pointing at all the boys telling Betsy to stay away from them because they're trouble, and doing that 'I'm watching you' thing with his fingers to any poor lad who dares to look our way.

Actually, all I can wish for in the future is that one day Betsy will find a young man who will love her and treat her like the special girl she is. I count my blessings every day that I have found someone as fabulous as Lee to spend the rest of my life with and I now look back at all the time I wasted on bad boys and commitment-phobes and put it down to experience. It's crazy to think that one day I may be watching my little baby get married and no doubt blubbing uncontrollably. But as a mum that's all you hope for – that your little one will grow up to have a happy, fulfilled life and to find love for themselves. That's what it's all about, isn't it?

As for adding to our brood? Lee and I chat quite often about whether we should try for another baby. I've always imagined having two children, as has Lee, who is really close to his brother. I'd always said that if I were to have two children I would ideally like them to be no more than three years apart so that they could grow up together and help each other out along the way. Some days we decide it's a good idea and then the next day when Betsy is racing around screaming at the top of her lungs we'll do a U-turn and wonder what the hell we were thinking. Of course, I'm not getting any younger which is always an important factor to consider for health reasons, and I certainly don't fancy being the oldest mum at the school gates. Who knows – if Betsy has a week of being as good as gold, maybe we'll be tempted. Watch this space...

A word from my Twitter followers

Annmarie, mum to a two-year-old daughter

My youngest has just hit the terrible twos! She does whatever she likes and thinks she can get away with it. She's very stubborn and even the private nursery she goes to has commented on how defiant she is if she doesn't want to do something. She has perfected the phrase 'I don't want to', and she means it! The naughty step is used but she doesn't take it seriously and has been known to fall asleep on it rather than say sorry.

Nicola, mum of two

My best piece of advice to anyone dealing with a crazed two-year-old is to ALWAYS keep your eyes on them! I once walked into my kitchen to see my dog not looking very amused. When I looked round the back of him (he is a big dog), my two-year-old was trying to put his finger in the dog's bottom! I've never scrubbed his hands so hard!

Claire, mum of three

When Nathan was going through his terrible twos, he was like a child possessed! Nathan was eleven months old when his twin sisters were born, which meant he learned to grow up very quickly. He was walking from a year old. He was putting his own plate in the kitchen when he was finished, helping me tidy away his toys – a proper little angel. And then one day it changed – he would cry all the time, shout, scream, throw things about. He became very jealous of his sisters, to the point where he would purposely take the toy they were playing with and hold it out of reach. With this complete disregard for others also came a very inquisitive side, which would often lead to mischief such as a Kit-Kat in the video player! He once threw an entire tub of talc all over my PC and left little white footprints all over my blue carpet leading back to his bed! Thankfully he grew out of it and has gone on to be a great role model for his younger siblings. Maybe the body snatchers felt sorry for me and returned my blue-eyed boy?

Ally, mum of two daughters

My first daughter's terrible twos started at eighteen months but the very mild tantrums were hardly terrible. I thought the terrible twos were over-exaggerated until my second daughter came along. Miranda was a whole new ball game. Her terrible twos started at eighteen months too but lasted until she was three and a half. She's still a stroppy madam now, age four, although I can read the warning signs more easily now.

Sara, mum to a three-year-old daughter

My daughter started playgroup in September and, after a few weeks of finding her feet, I was called in by the owner to be told she had pinched another kid. This then began a regular pattern: every Tuesday and Friday I would be told she had either pinched someone, poured water over another child's head or clawed someone on their face! I was mortified. After lots of guidance from the nursery and a new regime of taking away her favourite toys as punishment, she started to get better. I even asked the health visitor for advice. She said that lots of stress at home could be the reason why she was playing up, as she would pick up on it. I do believe stress is a big thing for a child and they are cleverer than we think.

Ali, mum to a four-year-old

My sister-in-law told me, 'You think the terrible twos are bad? Wait until you hit the terrible threes!' How right she was! The twos were a doddle in comparison!

Glen, dad of two daughters aged three and six

My Catholic wife decided we were all going to church this Christmas Eve, so we got there early to get the girls settled. After the first sermon by the young priest it went quiet and my two-year-old daughter Emma stood up and shouted, 'You cheeky bogger!' at the top of her voice. Needless to say the wife wasn't too happy and sent us to the car for the rest of the service!

Acknowledgements

Huge thanks to everyone involved in putting this book together.

A special thanks to my agents Claire Dundas at James Grant and Gordon Wise at Curtis Brown.

Sam Mann for spending hours listening to my stories and making sense of them.

Emma Tait at Headline Publishing and editor Lindsay Davies.

Jacket designer Nikki Dupin, text designer Dan Newman and illustrator Sam Wilsonhey.

And all my Twitter followers who have been so supportive and have shared their fabulous stories so you can enjoy them.

Thanks to Very, part of Shop Direct, the home shopping retailer.

Of course the book wouldn't be possible without my wonderful family. Lee and Betsy, I love you very much.

Betsy would like to thank her fabulous grandparents, Nanny and Granddad Mead and Nanny and Granddad Outen, as well as Godmother Elicia, Godfather Ross and Uncle Casey. She would also like to thank Mummy's friends Juju (Julie B) and Mama (Tamara), and her cousins Sunny, Freja, Sophie and Cameron.

She loves you all very much!